AN EXORCIST SPEAKS:

HOW TO RECOGNIZE AND PROTECT ONESELF AGAINST THE SNARES OF THE EVIL ONE

D1097167

Mons. Milivoj Bolobanic

Foreward by Fr. Gabriel Amorth

Translated from the Croatian.

Throughout the book, the words "man," "men," "mankind," "he," ""his," "himself," "brothers," "sons," etc. are denoted as being all-inclusive, respecting both genders, as the context requires.

Published by:
Ave Maria Centre of Peace,
P.O. Box 489, Station U, Toronto, ON, M8Z 5Y8 Canada
P.O. Box 375, Niagara Falls, NY 14304-0375 USA

ISBN #978-1-927108-10-9

Printed and bound in Canada by Ave Maria Centre of Peace

Prayer to St. Michael the Archangel

Saint Michael the Archangel, defend us in battle. Be our protection against the wickedness and snares of the devil. May God rebuke him, we humbly pray; and do Thou, O Prince of the Heavenly Host, by the Divine Power of God cast into hell Satan and all the evil spirits, who roam throughout the world, seeking the ruin of souls. Amen.

"These are the ones who have survived the great period of trial; they have washed their robes and made them white in the blood of the Lamb. It was this that brought them before God's throne: day and night they minister to him in his temple; he who sits on the throne will give them shelter. Never again shall they know hunger or thirst, nor shall the sun or its heat beat down on them, for the Lamb on the throne will shepherd them. He will lead them to springs of life-giving water, and God will wipe every tear from their eyes." (Rev. 7:14-17)

"I will put enmity between you and the woman, and between your offspring and hers." (Gen. 3:15)

"A great sign appeared in the sky, a woman clothed with the sun, with the moon under her feet, and on her head a crown of twelve stars." (Rev. 12:1)

All the quotes in this book are taken from the New American Bible, sponsored by the Bishops' Committee of the Confraternity of Christian Doctrine, U.S. Conference of Catholic Bishops.

Table of Contents

Foreward

I read the book of Monsignor Bolobanic with great pleasure and I am happy for the success which the book gained immediately after its printing. Today there are many books that speak of the Evil One and his actions.

Considering the fact that many people don't read much today, we need a short book to express, in a simple and clear way, what is important. How can we recognize the snares of the Evil One that are widespread today? We cannot close our eyes before this sad reality: never before in the Old Continent has faith lived in the midst of such apostasy. There exists a mathematical relation: as faith diminishes, superstition increases. Thus it is our people who have left the Church and are turning to witch doctors, fortune tellers, card readers and false clairvoyants; it is our people who have abandoned the life of Christian prayer and the sacraments and are turning to occult activities, especially spiritual séances and satanic sects, totally oblivious to the fatal consequences of these practices not only for their eternal life but also for their earthly life. They experience harsh disturbances which doctors are not able to recognize or treat. It is necessary to open people's eyes. Unfortunately, we have to admit that today not even the priesthood has been sufficiently familiarized with and is not completely immersed in the faith. Consequently, the clergy are barely capable of understanding or helping those seeking a way out of the darkness of the occult.

Therefore, with great pleasure I welcome this concise overview. I recommend it to priests as well as lay people, especially those in the field of education and those working with youth groups. Topics discussed in this book are among the most important, the most fundamental and the most useful to know.

The interview with the author at the end of the book is powerful. It has fulfilled its objective by providing answers from personal experience to the most frequently asked questions. And the choice of prayers in the book is very useful. Let us not forget that the foundation of everything and, in fact, the most effective prevention against the snares of the Evil One, is to live continuously in the grace of God, in prayer, to participate in the Mass and to receive the sacraments. It is always good to keep in mind Jesus' words: *"signs [like these] will accompany those who have professed their faith: they will use my name to expel demons."* (Mk. 16:17) According to these words we can all pray prayers of deliverance which, if prayed with faith, have the power of complete deliverance from the influence of the Evil One and evil actions.

Don Gabriele Amorth

Exorcist of the Diocese of Rome

Founder of the International Association of Exorcists

Introduction

T he territory of Satan's activity, his snares and seductions, the territory of occult and magic practices, is immeasurable. It is a precarious undertaking to venture into the field of satanic activity, so much of which is secret, neither understandable nor explainable. Consequently, the area remains largely unexplored.

Few people in our part of the world [Croatia] have attempted to penetrate this dark reality. Literature on the subject consists mainly of translations from foreign authors. Only with the light from above is it possible to discern, uncover and expose the snares of the Evil One. Only the Holy Spirit, the Spirit of wisdom, can enlighten and lead man through this dark, mysterious reality in which evil spirits move and operate. Only the Holy Spirit can discover the perfidious, perverted malice with which the evil spirits attack man in order to destroy him physically and mentally.

I have recognized that I have a certain sensitivity and openness towards human problems that are rooted in satanic influence. That area started to interest me a long time ago. Over the several decades of my pastoral work I have been delving deeper and deeper into this problem. Many people have come and more people are coming still, looking for help and a way out of their difficult and complex situations. And so, coming into contact with people, listening and trying to comprehend their problems, I penetrated deeper into the matter and began to grasp the mode and method of how Satan operates and seduces souls. I've realized clearly that he manipulates people in every possible way and that these unfortunate souls are not even aware of how they are victims of foul satanic practices.

For many years, a desire grew in me to educate and to point out to people the possible dangers they might fall into, especially if they were involved in the occult or magic practices. From late in the 20th century, evil has gained much ground, and satanic activity is on the increase, often unawares, even within the borders of our homeland. Many people fall into the snares of the devil without seeing a way out. Prompted by their plight and of those who have been delivered already and freed from evil, I decided to write this book. I hope to help many people become aware of their personal problems, open up their eyes, and with the light of the Holy Spirit, enable them to recognize where to go and how to come to salvation.

I realize that this book will provoke many stormy reactions. I am aware that Satan, whose works are being unveiled this way, stripped of his prey, will become furious and will try to seduce people by using newly-designed instruments to make them incapable of becoming aware of the truth. However, I am convinced that we have to speak about it in public, whether one likes it or not, and to help people this way. I hope that those who are waiting for help from somewhere and are overwhelmed by their problems will properly understand this book. For them this book will be like a balm put upon their wounds, will give them hope that all is not lost, will be like a haven of refuge.

In the Church we are not aware of the seriousness of the problems which people face today. In his book "An Exorcist Tells His Story," the famous exorcist Gabriele Amorth makes a serious statement: "The Catholic Church today has forgone this particular mission entrusted to her and the people are no longer turning to God, but to Satan."

This serious evaluation has sprung from a desire to enlighten us. Priests, in general, are not inclined to get involved nor are they prepared to render this particular kind of service. In our schools of theology these questions are barely touched upon. So, how will the priests of tomorrow cope with the evil invasion that threatens mankind to such a terrifying extent? It is time that we came to our senses and did something about it!

I place my modest contribution under the powerful protection of the Immaculate Virgin who is, according to God's design, Satan's perpetual enemy, and who will ultimately crush his head. The Triumph of the Immaculate Heart of Mary is imminent! Come, Lord Jesus! Maranatha! Destroy the power of Satan forever!

Man's Questions

Today man has many difficult and unsolved questions before him: Where does evil come from and why are felonies perpetrated in this world? Why do we have wars and why are brutal atrocities being committed against people? Why is there such a callous destruction of everything which man has laboriously achieved? Why is there so much hatred among nations as well as in the relationships among men? Why is there so much retaliation and revenge reaching the level of total extermination? Is it possible to explain bestial cruelty towards innocent victims — the massacre of women, the elderly and innocent children? And why are there so many incidences of rape? And all these things are happening in the 20th and 21st centuries!

Why is there so much social injustice in the modern and civilized world? Why do so many people die of hunger when so much food is being thrown away? Why does a minority on this planet possess enormous material goods while the majority lacks the basic necessities to live a dignified life?

Why does every country today spend enormous amounts of money to accumulate arms while many are dying of hunger? Why do we have weapons at all?

What could we say about tragedies and evils occurring on a personal level? It is hard to find a happy and contented person today, and it is almost impossible to encounter a happy family living in harmony. Frequent disagreements, marital infidelities, an increasing number of divorces, drug and alcohol abuse, homosexuality, many kinds of sexual perversions, more and more severe mental disorders and perversities ... all these incidents have become daily occurrences in the lives of many families and individuals.

Therefore, it is quite normal that man asks these questions: Where does evil in the world come from? Is there a way, or even a possibility, for man to step out of this vicious circle of evil events which is tightening its grip around us more and more every day? Is there a way of deliverance from all this?

Man has been asking these crucial questions from the day he came into this world, and the greatest thinkers of mankind have tried to come up with some answers. Philosophers, psychologists, moralists, writers, film producers, various analysts, the founders of different religions and religious movements — all have been engaged in dealing with these issues. None, however, has succeeded in providing satisfactory answers to these fundamental human questions and fewer have found a way to free man from this vicious circle of evil.

Human wisdom and man's intellect don't have the answers to these questions. Experience teaches us that suffering is part of our life from the cradle to the grave. Ever since man was put on this earth, all human effort has been directed to the creation of a paradise on earth. Despite this, we have to conclude, with anguish, that at the beginning of the 21st century, we still find ourselves living in a 'valley of tears.'

Man is to blame for many evils. However, there are other evils that we suffer, independent of our human will. These evils, for example, are various kinds of natural disasters: huge floods that leave enormous devastated areas behind, hail that destroys the crops and harvests, hurricanes and cyclones that destroy everything in their path, volcanoes and large earthquakes that erase whole cities and villages, even complete regional areas with all their population.

And what can we say about different kinds of fatal and incurable diseases? There are many patients lying in modern hospitals with no hope of ever being healed. How can one explain and account for the birth of so many handicapped children, disabled in their bodies or their minds, some of whom are in such a condition through the neglect of their parents?

How can one explain that in our 'advanced century' hundreds of thousands of people have had to leave their homes and countries carrying all their possessions in plastic bags, trying to find shelter under tents, if they were lucky enough to find one, with only minimal sanitary conditions? And yet they are happy to be alive. In addition, we must not overlook various types of moral and spiritual sufferings that torment and afflict human hearts. It would be enough just to mention here poor orphaned children who will never experience the meaning of motherly love and tenderness in their lives. We can also mention the pain that tears a parent's heart while in mourning for his or her dead child.

In most cases all of these evils and human troubles don't have their source in human faults, at least not visibly so. However, there are countless problems and anxieties that are obviously rooted in the evil lurking in the human heart.

Pride, selfishness, envy, jealousy, hatred, impurity and other evil inclinations are generated in the human heart. In most cases these roots have given birth to crimes, wars and countless other evils which have left behind barren wastelands and burnt sites in the course of human history. It all began with the murder of innocent Abel who was the victim of his brother's envy. We can confirm, with pain in our hearts, that the whole of human history is marked with trails of blood and suffering.

Yes, modern man is proud of the enviable progress he has made. Despite this fact, are we to say that contemporary man is happier than the man who lived a thousand years ago? Indeed, we truly enjoy some benefits of modern technological development, but are there not some new evils emerging on the horizon trailing along with this same progress? If it is so, then it is true what E. Autexier said: "To think that we can eradicate suffering from our lives means to toy with an illusion!"

God the Creator

God's revelation as contained in the Bible tells us without any doubt that God is the maker of the visible and invisible world. This is clearly confirmed in the Nicene Creed, formulated in Nicaea in 325, in which the Church professes: "We believe in one God, the Father Almighty, Maker of heaven and earth, and of all things visible and invisible..."

The fourth Lateran Council defined that God "from the beginning of time made at once out of nothing both orders of creatures, spiritual and corporeal, that is, the angelic and the earthly, and then the human creature, who, as it were, shares in both orders, being composed of spirit and body."

Out of these clearly-defined truths it follows that God first created spiritual, non-corporeal creatures that Sacred Scripture calls angels. These spiritual creatures are endowed with intelligence and free will. According to the Creator's design they constantly praise God and serve Him in carrying out His plan of salvation for other creatures. Saint Thomas Aquinas says: "Angels cooperate in everything that is good for us."

Satan

If God is a perfect being, it inevitably poses upon us this question: how is it possible that besides God, who is a perfect being, there is a completely corrupted being — Satan? Did God create Satan? This would go against God's perfection, so how is it possible that Satan exists?

The answer to these questions is given in the last book of the New Testament — in the Apocalypse or the Revelation of John the Apostle, where we read: *"Then war broke out in heaven; Michael and his angels battled against the dragon. Although the dragon and his angels fought back, they were overpowered and lost their place in heaven. The huge dragon, the ancient serpent known as the devil or Satan, the seducer of the whole world, was driven out; he was hurled down to earth and his minions with him. Then I heard a loud voice in heaven say: 'Now have salvation and power come, the reign of our God and the authority of his Anointed One. For the accuser of our brother is cast out, who night and day accused them before our God. They defeated him by the blood of the Lamb and by the word of their testimony; love for life did not deter them from death. So rejoice, you heavens, and you that dwell therein! But woe to you, earth and sea, for the devil has come down upon you! His fury knows no limits, for he knows his time is short.'"* (Rev. 12:7-12)

From this biblical account we see that there was a battle among the angels. Obviously, God created angels as inherently good. Being endowed with the gift of free will they had the ability to choose either good or evil. They were put to the test as to whether they would acknowledge God as their supreme Lord in obedience and love and freely offer themselves to His service. But pride sprang up among some of the angels with a desire to be God. Pride is a sin of the spirit. Lucifer, the angel of light, the most perfect of God's creation, together with a number of angels that followed him, refused to obey God. From that moment, they became evil spirits — demons. At the very moment when Lucifer, Satan, rebelled against God with his whole being and of his own volition, fully consciously and irrevocably, he became the creature who stands at the furthest distance from God. This sinful act of disobedience remained etched in his innermost being and will remain so throughout eternity. The Bible calls him by different names: Satan,

Lucifer, Beelzebub, the Ancient Serpent, the Devil, the Father of lies, and the Accuser of brothers …

Therefore, God did not create Satan and evil spirits; on the contrary, it is they who, through their own act of rebellion, consciously and freely, became evil. Notwithstanding this fact, Satan still possesses all the power and ability that he had been given before the rebellion took place. He remains a pure spirit and, therefore, a spiritual being who has unimaginable abilities, since he has lost none of his angelic nature. We must keep in mind that, as a pure spirit, he cannot be contained within the limits of our dimensions. Thus he is not "three — or four — dimensional," and consequently does not depend on the limits of time, substance (matter), sound, measures, food, rest, sickness or death. As a matter of fact, he is not subject to any of our human conditions. Of all his abilities, Satan uses that of exceptional knowledge in his hatred towards God and towards those who wish to serve God freely. He is the enemy who attacks and harasses in order to achieve his goal.

Demons hate God who is all goodness. They hate light because they themselves are all darkness and deception. They come from hell and overflow the earth, building their nests everywhere. Mostly they strive to penetrate the spirit and body of a human, to overshadow and overcome man by casting him into eternal destruction. Unfortunately, Christians today are not particularly aware of this horrible reality and even less so of whatever danger these malicious forces represent. Therefore they may easily fall into eternal damnation.

In the account of Revelation we know that Satan has already been judged and driven out (cf. Jn. 12:31) and that he has no authority whatsoever over Christ who defeated him through His Sacrifice on the Cross and His Resurrection and to whom — as the King of the universe and of all creation — everything will be gradually submitted, whether in heaven or on earth. Even so, Satan has been given more time to seduce people, holding this world under his evil authority, for he is called *"the Prince of this world."* (Jn. 14:30) Hence, to deny the existence of Satan and his negative actions in the world, means, in effect, to deny Christ and His salvific action that is continued effectively through His Bride, the Church, throughout history. For it is Christ who gave an explicit command to His Church "to drive out demons." So all those who deny the existence of Satan are doing him a big favor, allowing him to relentlessly operate in this world. Such believers and priests are true heretics, for believing in his existence is one of the tenets of our faith.

On the first Sunday of Lent in 2002 during the Angelus, Pope John Paul II spoke with a trembling voice to the faithful about the reality of Satan's existence that continually influences the ways of man and the Church. Those wishing to minimize the significance of this fact put themselves in danger and will eventually experience bitter disappointment; it is a mistake with painful consequences. The Pope concluded his address in an unusual way by emphatically saying twice these words: "BEGONE, SATAN!"

Some people tend to belittle Satan, talking scornfully about him and ridiculing him. One exorcist gave a lucid remark to such reactions: "Do not laugh, my friends, when you hear people talking about the Devil as a scarecrow for children! The Devil is pleased at such scorning for it is to his advantage, and very much so!"

The Creation of Man

Sacred Scripture recounts the story of the creation of the visible world with all its richness, diversity and order. God's almighty Word drew the world out of nothing so that it can be said that nothing exists that does not owe its existence to God the Creator. Man is the summit of God's work of creation.

God created man *"in his image."* (Gen. 1:27) Therefore, man holds a unique place in the whole order of creation. Somehow, both the spiritual and material worlds are united in man. Of all visible creation only man "is able to know and love his creator," (GS 12:3) and "he is the only creature on the earth that God has willed for its own sake." (GS 24:3) St. Catherine of Siena put it well: "What made you establish man in so great a dignity? Certainly it must be the incalculable love by which you have looked on your creature in yourself! You are taken with love for her; for by love indeed you created her, by love you have given her a being capable of tasting your eternal Good." (CCC, 356)

When God creates He creates only goodness. Thus the first man was established in friendship with his Creator and in harmony with himself and with the created world that was around him. The Church teaches us that God constituted man in a state of holiness and original justice. God created man in His own image and entrusted the whole world to his care. Man was given the grace to serve only the Lord and to be the governor of all creation.

The Fall of Man

Man could have lived happily if he abandoned himself freely to the will of God, for man depends on his Creator. But the fallen angel Satan, the Devil, tempted the first man out of envy and succeeded in shaking man's trust in the Creator. He persuaded man to use his freedom in the wrong way and induced him to break God's command. Seduced by the devil, man wanted to be like God. In fact, he chose himself over God.

The consequences of this primeval event that took place at the dawn of human history were fatal for our first parents and for the whole human race. The Bible clearly illustrates how the history of mankind is marked by the fallen act of our first parents. Immediately they lost the grace of their original holiness and began fearing God; the harmony that governed their inner being was disrupted, together with their ability to master spiritual powers of the soul over their bodies. From that moment on, the relationship between man and woman was marked by lust, with one overpowering the other; the whole domain of relationship with all other creatures was essentially disrupted to the extent that man started perceiving them as alien and hostile. The most difficult consequence which man had to accept was the fact of his imminent return unto the dust from where he came. Thus, through the sin of the first man, death entered into the history of mankind. Adam's sin was passed on to all his descendants and on to all generations. This is how Paul describes this truth: *"Just as through one man's disobedience all became sinners;"* (Rom. 5:19) *"Therefore, just as through one man sin entered the world and with sin, death, death thus coming to all..."* (Rom. 5:12) The Second Vatican Council expounds further by saying: "What divine revelation makes known to us agrees with experience. Examining his heart, man finds that he has inclinations toward evil, too, and is engulfed by manifold ills that cannot come from his good Creator. Often refusing to acknowledge God as his beginning, man has disrupted also his proper relationship to his own ultimate goal as well as his whole relationship toward himself and others and all created things." (Gaudium et spes (GS) 13)

There is no sensible answer to the original questions from the beginning of our reflection — where does evil come from, and why is there vast poverty which bears down heavily on the people of all times?; where does death come from? — unless we intertwine everything to the core of Adam's first sin. The truth of our faith teaches us that we are all infected, at birth, with Original Sin. Our forefather, Adam, received the grace of original holiness and justice, not only for himself but for the whole human race. Therefore, the sin of our first parents contaminates all of human nature and, by way of genealogy, it passes on to their descendants. Consequently, we say that human nature has been wounded, which means it is subject to ignorance and suffering, prone to sin and governed by lust. Through Adam's sin, Satan was given a range of authority over man who, despite this fact, remains free in his essence. Satan is very powerful because he is a pure spirit, though he still remains only a creature. His influence on individuals as well as on the whole of human society is immense, and he often causes enormous damage to both the spiritual and the physical nature, causing additional serious misconceptions in the field of education, politics, social activity and morals. John calls this fallen condition of mankind *"the sin of the world,"* (Jn. 1:29) denoting, with this expression, the influence of the Evil One on individuals as well as on communities and on our social structures, which bear the fruits of human sin.

This is how Vatican II describes the present dramatic state of the world that is *"all under the power of the Evil one"* (cf. 1 Jn. 5:19): "For a monumental struggle against the powers of darkness pervades the whole history of man. The battle was joined from the very origins of the world and will continue until the last day, as the Lord has attested." (See Mt. 24:13; 13:24-30 and 36-43) "Caught in this conflict, man is obliged to wrestle constantly if he is to cling to what is good, nor can he achieve his own integrity without great efforts and the help of God's grace." (GS 37)

Accordingly, Satan is not an idea but an entity who has powers and intelligence surpassing those of man and who operates in a concrete way; the only meaning for his existence is the envy of goodness. His activity regarding man did not end with the act in which he had played the agent in mankind's greatest tragedy at the beginning of human history. HE CONTINUES TO BE THE RELENTLESS AND LETHAL ADVERSARY OF MAN.

The New Adam and the New Eve

After Man's fall at the dawn of human history, it seemed as if the human race was in a dead-end situation. But on the very first pages in the Bible, right after the sin of our first parents, God still gives hope to mankind. God will not leave man forsaken and abandoned to the forces of the Evil One but, in some way, He gives us certain indications regarding His plan of salvation which will reach its fulfillment in due time. We read these important words: *"I will put enmity between you and the woman, and between your offspring and hers; He will strike at your head, while you strike at his heel."* (Gen. 3:15)

Contemplating this text throughout the course of her rich history, the Church discovers in it God's plan of salvation. By Adam's disobedience, mankind fell deep and low. However, when the New Adam, Jesus Christ, comes, He will amend the guilt of the old Adam through his obedience to death on the cross (Phil. 2:8) — *"he will save his people from their sins"* (Mt. 1:21) — and destroy the works of the devil. Jesus Christ is the New Adam, the Head of redeemed mankind. John phrases it in this way: *"Of his fullness we have all had a share — love following upon love."* (Jn. 1:16)

As for the Virgin Mary, she is granted an immediate share in God's plan of salvation through her complete surrender to the will of God, through her faith freely accepted and her absolute obedience to Him. She said her 'YES' (FIAT) to God in the name of the whole human race and thus, through her act of obedience, became the New Eve, the Mother of the living.

According to God's eternal design, the Church anticipates a time of cleansing when the Virgin will crush the Serpent's head. Then the restored Church, with the whole of humanity, will experience a radiant morning light that has never been seen before. A time of peace and justice will be the answer to all the assaults from hell against miserable mankind, the object of all forces of evil. However, before all this happens there will be the last battle between light and darkness, love and hatred, good and evil, life and death.

Christ and Satan

In alignment with God's plan, Jesus Christ has a central part in creation and in its redemption, for all things were created, *"through him and for him."* (cf. Col. 1:16) The Bible tells us much about the Kingdom of God as well as about the kingdom of Satan; of the power and strength of God, the Lord of the Universe, but also of the power of darkness; furthermore, it speaks of the sons of God, but also of the sons of Satan. Therefore, it is impossible to comprehend Christ's redemptive act and not realize at the same time the destructive act of Satan.

Jesus came into this world *"to destroy the devil's works,"* (1 Jn. 3:8) to deliver man from Satan's bondage and to establish the Kingdom of God after having destroyed the kingdom of Satan.

Satan was a murderer of men from the beginning; (cf. Jn. 8:44) he is the Adversary, the Tempter, the Accuser, by whom evil, pain, sin and death entered into this world. Jesus calls him *"the prince of this world."* (cf. Jn. 14:30) Paul speaks of him as *"the god of the present age;"* (2 Cor. 4:4) John claims that *"the whole world is under the evil one."* (1 Jn. 5:19)

It is necessary here to point out distinctly the error of a number of modern theologians, which they share with many others, that is the denial of the existence of Satan. They reckon that Satan is some abstract concept and advise us not to be frightened of Satan because he doesn't exist. When the Bible gives accounts of evil spirits, it describes them as personal beings endowed with faculties like reason, will, freedom, and venturesome spirit. This fact is confirmed by the patristic tradition as well as by the Magisterium of the Church. Therefore, whoever denies Satan, denies sin, and consequently does not comprehend the redemptive work of Christ.

Satan is indeed powerful and his power is dangerous since he is primarily a seducer, and a liar, lurking treacherously at the same time. He doesn't like to be unmasked and exposed. Someone astutely noticed this and wrote it down: "Satan's greatest guile is to convince us he does not exist," which is quite understandable. For if he has made us believe that he does not exist, we won't count him as a real entity in our lives any more, after which Satan can lead us by the nose and pull a fast one on us for being blind to this fact. He can stir up personal, social and family conflicts, riots across the world, whirling up terrible tyrannies and violence. It is evident how successful he has been in his actions today.

The Gospels attribute much importance to the direct conflict between Christ and Satan, emphasizing the absolute defeat of Satan. In order for us to understand the great power Jesus exerted over Satan, it is important to look more closely at some sentences that are written in Sacred Scripture. Thus John in his epistle says: *"It was to destroy the devil's works that the Son of God revealed himself,"* (1 Jn. 3:8) and Peter, wishing to explain in brief the works of Christ to Cornelius, a new convert from paganism, describes it like this: *"He went about doing good works and healing all who were in the grip of the devil, and God was with him."* (Acts 10:38) And finally, when Paul explains the nature of the battle which a Christian has to endure and remain persistently faithful to Christ, he says: *"Put on the armor of God so that you may be able to stand firm against the tactics of the devil. Our battle is not against human forces but against the principalities and powers, the rulers of this world of darkness, the evil spirits in regions above."* (Eph. 6:11-12)

The Temptations in the Desert

At the very beginning of Jesus' public life, immediately after the solemn proclamation from the Father at the River Jordan, Satan approached Jesus to tempt him. Jesus had withdrawn into the solitude of the desert to fast and pray for forty days and nights. He was clearly ready to confront the traps of the Evil One, having been in the most intimate union with his Father, in self-denial and penance.

FIRST TEMPTATION

The first trap of the tempter was, *"If you are the Son of God, command these stones to turn into bread."* (Mt. 4:3) Jesus replied: *"Scripture has it: 'Not on bread alone is man to live but on evey utterance that comes from the mouth of God.'"* (Mt. 4:4) There is no doubt that the tempter, according to his own vision, made every effort to choose the right moment when Jesus was physically exhausted.

When a person is worn out and hungry it is quite normal for him to crave food. However, we should wisely recognize this as a trap of the devil, about whom we should always be vigilant.

In reality, many sins that we commit begin in such a manner: avarice, small surrenders to sensual feelings, indulging in physical pleasure... and all this is done under the guise of "permissible," which is often followed by the attempt to justify it: "Well, everyone is doing it, everybody is behaving like this!" And Satan is so cunning. He doesn't want to manifest or reveal himself immediately; he does not want us to recognize him as the fallen angel in the state of disobedience, but, on the contrary, he greatly enjoys presenting himself as the angel of light, merciful, compassionate, sympathetic. He suggested that Christ, who is exhausted with hunger, eat to appease His hunger. What could be more natural than that? But it is not about that. Christ is God and He perceives the hidden danger, whereby man runs the risk of neglecting his spirit because of the needs of his body. Today, so many people think only of how to satisfy their appetites and their sensual passions, leaving their souls empty, void of the presence of God. Jesus could have performed the miracle, like the one recorded on two occasions in the Gospels, when He multiplied loaves of bread and fed thousands of people. In this case, however, Jesus was facing a sly trap. That is why his reply was categoric, determined, not relenting whatsoever: *"...Not on bread alone is man to live, but on evey utterance that comes from the mouth of God."* (Mt. 4:4)

SECOND TEMPTATION

We must know that Satan never thinks of himself as defeated, so he tempted Jesus for the second time. When his first trap failed, he invited Jesus to climb up to the top of the Jerusalem Temple and there said to Him: *"If you are the Son of God, throw yourself down. Scripture has it: 'He will bid his angels take care of you; with their hands they will support you that you may never stumble on a stone.'"* (Mt. 4:6) In this second attempt we find a two-fold trap. The sin of vanity is hidden behind Satan's words. He suggested that Jesus perform a sensational action before an audience, a deadly jump for which He would have received applause and admiration from everyone.

People crave sensational and extraordinary events. People want to identify with their idols: singers, actors, athletes. People today resemble those of ancient Rome, "desirous of bread and circuses." In this second temptation, Jesus' reply was the same as in the first case, that is, sharp, determined, and without compromise. He answered the tempter: *"Again it is written, 'You shall not put the Lord, your God, to the test.'"* (Mt. 4:7) If Jesus had gratified the tempter, it would have meant a shift in roles; in other words it would have meant that creature would have been given the role of the Creator. Satan was outraged and furious because he had failed for the second time to persuade Jesus to act upon his proposal to perform a miracle.

THIRD TEMPTATION

The tempter then launched the third and most hideous attack. Satan wanted to entice Jesus to commit a sin to bring about the ruin of man for the whole of eternity: *"The devil then took him up a very high mountain and displayed before him all the kingdoms of the world in their magnificence, promising 'All these will I bestow on you if you prostrate yourself in homage before me.' At this, Jesus said to him, "Away with you, Satan! Scripture has it: 'You shall do homage to the Lord your God; him alone shall you adore."""* (Mt. 4:8-10) There is such folly in Satan. He fantasizes that everything belongs to him, whereas, in fact, he owns nothing! He promises many things to men — success, glory, popularity, power, riches, happiness, progress and pleasure — which he ultimately takes away, leading men to the verge of an abyss. His continual strategy is to convince man that everything is ruined. Life is meaningless, worthless and there is only one decision left for a man to make, that is, to take his own life. Are we not today the witnesses of more frequent suicidal incidences, especially in young people?

Jesus repudiated Satan's third temptation very convincingly: *"Away with you, Satan! Scripture has it: 'You shall do homage to the Lord your God; him alone shall you adore.'"* (Mt. 4:10) The words of Jesus manifest such power and determination! A very important life message is hidden in those words for those who worship only idols or false gods such as money, pseudo-science, sensual pleasures, influence and power, career, publicity and prestige, drugs and alcohol....

All these temptations which Satan set before Jesus underline an actual well-concealed intention for us to accept the desires and longings of the body, the world and the devil who, through food, success, power and so on, wants to overpower the spirit. His purpose is to turn us away from God and destroy our souls. The Old Adam had chosen the promises of Satan whereas the New Adam, Christ, chose to obey God, even though it brought upon Him a terrible death on the cross.

Who would be able to count the number of souls Satan is holding today in his bondage, precisely by the power of these devices? All those who have put their trust in him end up seduced by his false promises and are now his slaves, bound in shackles, unaware and 'blind.' This is the reason why John named him three times as "the prince of this world." But Jesus came to us to destroy the power which the Evil One exerted over many who had believed in his perfidious enticements; Jesus came to crush down his power, to unbind the 'chains' of bondage by which the Devil kept man shackled, to set His beloved ones free and give them life. Jesus said to His disciples: *"Now has judgment come upon this world, now will this world's prince be driven out..."* (cf. Jn. 12:31)

Jesus and Evil Spirits in the Gospels

In the Synoptic Gospels the evangelists eagerly desired to single out the divinity of Christ in a particular way. Therefore their accounts relate especially the extraordinary signs and miracles that Jesus performed, among which they give special importance to Jesus' lordship over unclean spirits. It comes from the fact that Jesus' work is aimed at destroying the power of Satan and liberating mankind, as has been already mentioned.

Thus on three occasions Mark emphasizes this particular power of Christ: *"There appeared in their synagogue a man with an unclean spirit that shrieked: 'What do you want of us, Jesus of Nazareth? Have you come to destroy us? I know who you are — the holy One of God!' Jesus rebuked him sharply: 'Be quiet! Come out of the man!' At that the unclean spirit convulsed the man violently and with a loud shriek came out of him. All who looked upon were amazed. They began to ask one another: 'What does this mean? A completely new teaching in a spirit of authority! He gives orders to unclean spirits and they obey!'"* (Mk. 1:23-27) It is crucial to notice here the way people connect Jesus' preaching with His power and authority to drive out unclean spirits. *"Before long the whole town was gathered outside the door. Those whom he cured, who were variously afflicted, were many, and so were the demons he expelled. But he would not permit the demons to speak, because they knew him."* (Mk. 1:33-34) Likewise, it is important to observe that Jesus did not want any testimony whatsoever from the evil spirits since, in essence, they are liars and twisters of words. Jesus has testimony from the Father and He wants us to become His witnesses. Mark reported on this in the first chapter of his: *"So he went into their synagogues preaching the good news and expelling demons throughout the whole of Galilee."* (Mk. 1:39)

Matthew tells us how Jesus delivered many who were oppressed: *"... his reputation traveled the length of Syria. They carried to him all those afflicted with various diseases and racked with pain: the possessed, the lunatics, the paralyzed. He cured them all."* (Mt. 4:24) *"As evening drew on, they brought him many who were possessed. He expelled the spirits by a simple command and cured all who were afflicted."* (Mt. 8:16)

Luke gives similar reports: *"At sunset, all who had people sick with a variety of diseases took them to him and he laid hands on each of them and cured them. Demons departed from many, crying out as they did so, 'You are the Son of God.' He rebuked them and did not allow them to speak because they knew that he was the Messiah."* (Lk. 4:40-41) *"There were many of his disciples; a large crowd of people was with them from all Judea and Jerusalem and the coast of Tyre and Sidon, people who came to hear him and be healed of their diseases. Those who were troubled by unclean spirits were cured; indeed the whole crowd was trying to touch him because power went out of him which cured all;"* (Lk. 6:17-19) *"... and also some women who had been cured of evil spirits and maladies: Mary called Magdalene, from whom seven devils had gone out."* (Lk. 8:2)

We give special attention to two incidents that emphasize significant details. First we will consider the case of the possessed man from the Gerasenes region. In fact, this is the worst form of a complete demonic possession in which the possessed man displayed superhuman strength in such a way as to be able to tear off his own chains. In other cases of possession we do not see these manifestations. Sometimes evil can take the form of some physical illnesses, as in the case of the deaf and mute man or the crippled woman. Even today, we encounter various kinds of manifestations in possessed persons.

It is important to notice what the evil spirit answered when Jesus asked his name: *"'What is your name?' Jesus asked him. 'Legion is my name,' he answered. 'There are hundreds of us.'"* (Mk. 5:9) This happens today also. What is of note here is that Jesus gratified the plea of the evil spirits not to drive them away but to send them into a herd of pigs. The same thing occurs today when, during the Rite of Exorcism, the evil spirit begs the exorcist to send it here or there; again, the exorcist is authorized to determine the place to cast the evil spirits. It is also very significant to note that Jesus never commanded someone who had been possessed to be silent about his/her deliverance, which He did in cases of healing from infirmities.

The second example of possession is the account of the healing of a young man whom the apostles had not succeeded in delivering from the evil spirit while Jesus was on Mount Tabor with Peter, James and John. This is yet another example of a difficult case of possession. The demon was torturing the boy, throwing him on the ground, turning him rigid, and making him grind his teeth and foam at the mouth so that it seemed as if the boy was displaying signs of epilepsy. The evil spirit wanted to destroy the boy by casting him first into water and then into fire. The description of the incident was given by Luke (9:38-43) and Mark (9:14-27). Jesus had asked a concrete and meaningful question: "How long has this been happening to him?" And the boy's father said: "From childhood." The answer illustrates that the victim does not bear any guilt.

Jesus established certain conditions for the boy to be set free. In the first place, He asked the father to have faith: *"Everything is possible to a man who trusts."* (Mk. 9:23) And to His astounded disciples who were disappointed because of their failure He said: *"This kind you can drive out only by prayer (and fasting)."* (Mk. 9:29) This means that some cases of liberation from the evil spirits, particularly important and rather difficult in their nature, do not happen automatically and require not only faith but also prolonged prayer and fasting on the part of the exorcist.

When Jesus encountered the evil spirit in possessed persons, certain significant details were observed. These are given below:

• The evil spirit can enter a man, as in the case of Judas: *"He dipped the morsel, then took it and gave it to Judas, son of Simon Iscariot. Immediately after, Satan entered his heart."* (Jn. 13:26-27);

• After a person has been delivered, the evil spirit can return, bringing with him a host of others, even more evil spirits (Mt. 12:43-45);

• An evil spirit can perform amazing works to seduce people, as Simon Magus did (Acts 8:9);

• In certain times the evil spirit exerts special power: *"... but this is your hour - the triumph of darkness."* (Lk. 22:53);

• Satan will manifests these kinds of unique powers in the end times, as Jesus' eschatological utterances and the Book of Revelation clearly show.

The Evil Spirit is Enraged When it is Exposed and Beaten

In fear that people might start exalting Jesus, the Jews, together with their scribes and Pharisees, said: *"He casts out demons through the prince of demons."* (cf. Mt. 9:34) *"Now we are sure you are possessed."* (Jn. 8:52) *"'He is possessed by Beelzebub,'* and, *'He expels demons with the help of the prince of demons .*" (Mk. 3:22) Jesus provided three responses to these accusations.

His first rebuttal showed how much the first allegation is contradictory and meaningless in itself. *"Summoning them, he then began to speak to them by way of examples: 'How can Satan expel Satan? If a kingdom is torn by civil strife, that kingdom cannot last. If a household is divided according to loyalties, that household will not survive. Similarly, if Satan has suffered mutiny in his ranks and is torn by dissension, he cannot endure; he is finished.'"* (Mk. 3:23-26) Jesus' second rebuttal was stronger as He explained to His listeners: *"But if it is by the Spirit of God that I expel demons, then the reign of God has overtaken you."* (Mt. 12:28) And, *"Now has judgment come upon this world, now will this world's prince be driven out."* (Jn. 12:31)

In his third response, Jesus manifested His absolute supremacy and ultimate defeat of Satan: *"When a strong man, fully armed, guards his courtyard, his possessions go undisturbed. But when someone stronger than he comes and overpowers him, such a one carries off the arms on which he was relying and divides the spoils."* (Lk. 11:21-22) *"... the Prince of this world is at hand. He has no hold on me."* (Jn. 14:30)

Activity of Satan Today

We have already mentioned that Satan and his fallen angels, though separated from God, preserved their power and ranks (thrones, dominions, principalities, powers) and used this power and authority for evil purposes.

Between the first coming of Jesus to this world and the second coming on the Last Judgment Day, Satan is trying to win over as many souls as he can; his only purpose is the ruin and the destruction of men. St. Augustine affirms that if God had given Satan a free rein, *"not a human being would be saved."* (Mt. 24:22) Satan's cruelty is so intense that he would devour each of us in a blink of an eye, if God's protection were not over us. Clearly, Satan is in a big hurry. He knows that he has already been vanquished and *"knows his time is short."* (Rev. 12:12) Desperate creature that he is, he tries to lure as many people as he can. According to the Word of God, "The battle was joined from the very origins of the world and will continue until the last day." (GS 37)

Satan cannot attack God directly; he fights God by pouring on God's people all of his vengeful malice, hatred, envy and jealousy. And every man, without exception, engages in the battle. Our life on this earth is a continuous trial during which our faithfulness to God or our succumbing to the snares of the devil is being tested. At the end of our life, each of us will appear before the tribunal of God, to receive what we have merited according to our good and bad deeds. It is clearly obvious that Satan's power in certain periods of human history was manifested to a stronger or lesser extent, first in the life of a community, and subsequently in the lives of individuals. Thus many historians believe that the fall of the Roman Empire was a result of moral depravity which infected the whole society of that time. We can clearly see this in Paul's testimony in his Epistle to the Romans.

Many people perceive the world today, and particularly the West, to be in the same condition as it was in ancient Roman times. The Evil One tempts people with materialism, hedonism, and consumerism, promising them a paradise on this earth. Unfortunately, many

Christians haven't recognized the lures as perfidious lies and sly traps of the devil and so they rush headlong more and more into his cold embrace. The mass media are collaborators, often acting as agents in the service of the Evil One, spreading an atmosphere of materialism, hedonism and consumerism. Satan puts special emphasis today on the cult of sex, reducing the human body to an instrument of sin. This is what we call regular activities of Satan, otherwise called regular temptation to sin. Occurrences of these kind are many and they appear in varied forms. The Satanic propaganda is impertinent, diffused and overt, promoting satanic contents that have direct or indirect influence on men, destroying their lives and leading their souls to perdition.

Wherever the faith is repressed and chastity is violated, crime and iniquity are excused; wherever there are disputes causing divorce or violence, there Satan is involved. The activity of Satan and his minions encompasses the whole world. We should mention here Satan's continuous temptations of pride, haughtiness and envy extending over the entire world, in all areas of life — political, economic, and social. This is why Jesus says: *"The whole world is under the evil one,"* (1 Jn. 5:19) and no one can escape his grip but those who strive to live close to Jesus through the means He has given us: sacraments, fasting and prayer. Only those who observe these means can defeat Satan in his regular activity and will not fall victim to his extraordinary activities.

Extraordinary Activities of Satan

It is necessary to go over, and, in a particular way, to consider the so-called extraordinary activities of Satan which God, obviously, allows to occur in some exceptional cases.

Direct Physical Attacks of Satan

Biographies of great individuals in our Church — St. John of the Cross, the Curé of Ars, St. John Vianney, or St. Pio from Pietrelcina, Italy — demonstrate how they were harassed by evil spirits in an extraordinary way. The accounts talk of their sufferings, such as being whipped, battered or beaten by evil spirits. There are also good holy souls who, seriously engaged on their path to perfection, are persecuted and exposed to the attacks of Satan with God's permission. Their sufferings have become a means for reparation, purification and sanctification, and fulfillment of redemptive purposes. Whatever the source of their afflictions, it transforms into salvation if accepted with faith and with generous disposition in the spirit of sacrifice. It is very important to understand that, in these examples, Satan does not have any interior influence whatsoever on the person involved, and therefore there is no need to pray for deliverance or exorcism of these individuals.

These individuals are chosen by God to carry out special missions. Because of their complete devotion (adherence) to God's plans, they become exceptional charismatic instruments for the salvation of the world, but also targets of Satan's attacks of extraordinary fierceness, openness and directness, inflicting them with extreme sufferings. Satan wants to instill them with fear and turn them away from the mission that they have embraced from God. At the same time, the mystery and the presence of God's providence draw a greater good out of these torments. God gives permission to the evil spirit to act in an extraordinary way upon these virtuous people so that God's power, which dwells inside them, can be manifested to a greater extent.

Demonic Possession

This is the gravest form of satanic affliction on a person, whereby Satan takes full possession of the body of the victim but not the soul. The possessed then acts and speaks as Satan dictates. In cases such as these, the victim simply is not able to resist the evil spirit and consequently cannot be morally responsible for his actions or words. These types of possessions usually occur with spectacular phenomena such as: the possessed start talking in foreign languages, display a superhuman strength, tear iron chains apart, reveal secret things and even expose the thoughts of other people ... The Bible recalls for us the well-known case, as previously mentioned, of the demoniac from Gerasenes.

Experience has shown that in some individuals, the devil can control their bodily faculties at his will. Thus he can lift the body of a person into the air and hold it up for a long time, transfer it quite easily and swiftly from one place to another, make the victim speak ancient or modern languages unfamiliar to the victim, or have the victim recite unfamiliar passages by heart. Even some physiological functions of the body (digestion, secretion, blood circulation, breathing) can be modified by the devil.

Sometimes the body of the victim takes on various positions — it can easily imitate the movements of a skilled acrobat; walk or run with its eyes closed, dodging every obstacle; play an instrument or paint with excellence; and perform many other activities which the victim alone has never learned. Also, the victim may shout in a piercing voice, or recognize hidden events from the past with which he/she could not have been familiar. The person may be able to read another person's mind and perform other astonishing actions.

It should be noted that, in practice, there are many different types of possessions that vary in intensity, difficulty and symptoms. Therefore, it is not useful to pick out a single case and use it as a model to assess other cases. It should be said that cases of complete demonic possession are rather rare. Nevertheless, they happen even today and have a common characteristic manifested in the victims rejecting everything holy, which is usually followed by abhorrent swearing. We must always be on our guard and alert, for the evil spirit is known to disguise himself in order to deceive and divert our attention to something insignificant. Murders and suicides are often related to possessed individuals.

Demonic Harassment

This form of demonic activity includes various difficulties that individuals may experience caused by an evil spirit. We attach to this term various disturbances and diseases ranging in degree from slight to serious ones, which could eventually reach the point of becoming a real possession. Sometimes in these cases it can happen that the victim loses consciousness, or starts acting oddly or speaking some words for which he is not responsible.

In order for us to better understand these occurrences, we provide several examples from the Bible. In the Old Testament there is the example of the righteous Job who was not possessed by Satan, but suffered from grave maladies inflicted upon him by Satan, enduring the loss of his children and material possessions. In the New Testament, there is the peculiar case of the crippled woman and another case of a deaf mute person, both of whom Jesus delivered. They were not fully possessed by the evil spirit but his presence was felt strongly by them in their physical illnesses. As for St. Paul, he was not under the influence of Satan's power but was continuously tormented by him, as he described it himself: *"In order that I might not become conceited I was given a thorn in the flesh, an angel of Satan to beat me and keep me from being too proud."* (2 Cor. 12:7)

Although cases of full possession are rare, priests in their pastoral practice often encounter many individuals harassed by Satan who strikes at their health and material goods, blocks their daily activities and causes them emotional turmoil. Very often when priests come across these or similar occurrences, they have to determine what ominous cause brings about these problems. It often means that a priest is expected to be able to discern whether a certain disorder is of satanic origin or not, and if it is, how to remove it.

To be able to assess a situation, the priest must always keep in mind that each case is unique, and cases may display vast differences in symptoms, as well as the whole specter of distinctions related to the intensity of satanic disturbances. The forms may greatly vary: attack on one's health, difficulties and barriers at work, disorders in the person's feelings and sentiments, serious interruption in human relationships, strong unjustified anger, withdrawals or seclusion from one's surroundings, suicidal thoughts.

If a demonic harassment is not treated immediately by the means which God has given us, it will continue persistently and become a real and true demonic obsession, reducing the victim to an almost animal-like condition, destroying his neurovegetative system, his sleep and appetite. But, most often there is a continuous psycho-physiological decay of the victim.

I would like to mention a few examples of persons who go in and out of hospital with no medical diagnosis. Specialists may say that the patient's disease has reached its final stage but, at the same time, 'clinically' they are not able to find anything. The patient is fading psychologically and physiologically, cannot sleep, suffers from anorexia (the loss of appetite, a sense of nausea before meals), suffers constant and strong headaches, has continuous bloody diarrhea, and the patient's ability to hear and speak is diminished. Compare this to the case taken from the Bible of the deaf mute person who was possessed, who could speak and hear immediately after Jesus delivered him from the grip of Satan.

Demonic Obsession

Persons with these disturbances are often found to have obsessive, meaningless thoughts, of which they cannot rid themselves. Such a person experiences a division in his innermost being. Although his will is free, it is to a large extent under the pressure of obsessive and compulsive thoughts. We are dealing here with unexpected attacks, repetitive in nature, over a longer period of time. The obsessive thoughts are the reason why the afflicted person lives in a permanent state of exhaustion and depression, accompanied by temptations to commit suicide. Obsessive thoughts often have an impact on one's dreams.

When these problems happen, people understandably may think that the phenomenon belongs to the field of psychiatry. However, there are cases where all psychological, psychiatric and medical efforts cannot come up with either an explanation or help of any kind. Psychiatry, neurology, psychology and parapsychology are not capable of explaining these phenomena, as the subjects of analysis evade the instruments of testing and verification. Without a doubt, this is an indication of Satan's activity and presence, in which case science is helpless. It is possible for a priest to notice and discern it correctly, with the help of God's mercy, with which he (the priest) cooperates through prayer and a long devoted pastoral practice.

Demonic Infestation

Here we do not think of satanic activity directly affecting a person but a demonic infestation or disturbance of various premises (house, office, store, field…) as well as of different objects (beds, pillows, dolls, cars and similar objects, and sometimes animals). A well-known phenomenon is that of noise occurring in rooms, at any time of the day or night; lights appearing independently; sounds of completely unknown songs; objects carried away or furniture and chairs overthrown; mattresses turning into real beds of thorns and nails; plates, bottles and glasses breaking into pieces for no reason, without having been touched; doors and windows, although well-shut and without wind, suddenly opening or shutting; chairs freely moving all over the house on their own; water-pipes leaking blood instead of water, etc. Due to such satanic disturbances of matter, a family is not able to sleep and, because of fear and harassment from the demons, they inexplicably become ill. Often there are quite unusual illnesses, accompanied with severe pain that medical science is not able to detect.

All this may seem like a fabricated story but exorcists, who often come across such cases, bring out irrefutable facts based on their experience.

In his works, Origen relates that from the very first centuries of Christianity, the rite of exorcism was performed when such or similar cases occurred.

Subjugation to the Devil

This term denotes a voluntary personal act by which a person signs a contract with the devil. It is also known that a person can sign a blood covenant with Satan. Horrible and abominable scenes occur at so-called black masses. This phenomenon is spreading more and more today, and is very much present in our cities.

How Does One Fall Prey to Extraordinary Diabolic Activities?

It is of great importance for each person to know how one can become entangled in the extraordinary workings of the devil. If we take careful note of these activities, we will be able to understand what to do to receive deliverance by God in order to become free from Satan's grip. Following are four main ways that we can become involved in satanic activity.

With God's Permission

There isn't a single event happening on the world scene and in the life of every individual that is accidental, that is, without God's permission, for everything is under God's control: *"...yet not a hair of your head will be harmed."* (cf. Lk. 21:18) Since God has given us freedom, He allows the Evil One's actions, even though He never wishes them to happen. Even if God allows evil to act, He nevertheless draws out of it only good and uses it for the good. Although Satan originates as one of God's creation and is a pure spirit, like every other creature he cannot act in any way without God's permission. God sometimes allows Satan to act in order to punish us, sometimes to test our faithfulness, and at other times to kindle in us a true faith which we may have given up by living a worldly life. God can permit Satan to attack and molest us, but at the same time, He always provides every grace necessary to resist Satan. God speaks to us through Holy Scripture: *"If you choose, you can keep the commandments; it is loyalty to do his will."* (Sir. 15:15) Thus God allows us to turn our trials into a way of acquiring virtues for ourselves so that we can practise humility, patience and mortification.

Why doesn't God, who is immensely greater and more powerful than Satan, stop Satan's actions or confine him to Hell? God never takes away undeserved gifts from His creatures. Only we, through our own deeds, can lose these gifts, including God's grace, which was once lost, first by the unfaithful angels, and, after them, by man who misused the gift of free will. The natural endowments are preserved in spite of sin, for God draws good out of evil through His mysterious providence. The day will come when even Satan will have to admit that he has been serving God all along. Temptations with which Satan entices man often serve to make man more vigilant, prayerful, and to draw him nearer to God. God allows man to fall so that he may become aware of his own sinful nature and worthlessness. However, man should not dwell upon this, but repent for having offended God, who is infinite Love and Goodness. Furthermore, man must develop a hatred of sin, renounce it and fight against it. Only then can God's grace fall upon the soul and lift it up to Him.

Satan, who is unable to do good, will have to admit on Judgment Day that he has been working for God's glory and has contributed much to the salvation and glorification of many saints and martyrs, virgins and beatified triumphant in Heaven. Thus, in the life of some persons, God may permit the Evil One to act, so that in turn, it will produce much spiritual fruit. The actions of the Evil One had their purpose in all this, but God expunged evil actions to achieve His own purpose. This fact is most manifested in charismatic individuals who have been chosen by God for His service and endowed with many charismatic gifts, upon whom God allows agonies and extraordinary crosses to come. St. Pio suffered for 50 years from harsh and piercing pains. He bore the stigmata, that is, the same wounds as our Lord Jesus Christ had. Despite this, no one thought to start praying for Padre Pio in order for his wounds to disappear. It was perceived as an exceptional intervention by God that was obviously aimed to achieve a higher purpose. No doubt Satan did not see any advantage for himself in Padre Pio's bearing the stigmata, even though Satan can also cause such miraculous manifestations and thus deceive people with false mystics.

We have an example of this in the Bible. It is the account of the famous sufferer, Job, who was afflicted with many agonies and troubles, and who was ultimately stricken with the worst agony of all. Undoubtedly he is the most tempted person in human history. The Book of Job describes it this way: *"One day, when the sons of God came to present themselves before the LORD, Satan also came among them. And the LORD said to Satan, 'Whence do you come?' Then Satan answered the LORD and said, 'From roaming the earth and patrolling it.' And the LORD said to Satan, 'Have you noticed my servant Job, and that there is no one on earth like him, blameless and upright, fearing God and avoiding evil? But Satan answered the LORD and said, 'Is it for nothing* that Job is God-fearing? Have you not surrounded him and his family and all that he has with your protection? You have blessed the work of his hands, and his livestock are spread over the land. But now put forth your hand and touch anything that he has, and surely he will blaspheme you to your face.' And the LORD said to Satan, 'Behold, all that he has is in your power; only do not lay a hand upon his person.' So Satan went forth from the presence of the LORD."* (Job 1:6-12)

THE FIRST TRIAL

From this account it is evident that God permitted Satan to test Job, the faithful servant of God, and that Satan ultimately destroyed all his possessions — lands, houses, livestock, even his sons and daughters. However, in all these temptations, Job preserved his inner calm declaring: *"'Naked I came forth from my mother's womb, and naked shall I go back again. The LORD gave and the LORD has taken away; blessed be the name of the LORD!' In all this Job did not sin, nor did he say anything disrespectful of God."* (Job 1:21-22)

THE SECOND TRIAL

After that, God allowed a second temptation: *"Once again the sons of God came to present themselves before the LORD, and Satan also came with them. And the LORD said to Satan, 'Whence do you come?' And Satan answered the LORD and said, 'From roaming the earth and patrolling it.' And the LORD said to Satan, 'Have you noticed my servant Job, and that there is no one on earth like him, faultless and upright, fearing God and avoiding evil? He still holds fast to his innocence although you incited me against him to ruin him without cause.' And Satan answered the LORD and said, 'Skin for skin! All that a man has will he give for his life. But now put forth your hand and touch his bone and his flesh, and surely he will blaspheme you to your face.' And the LORD said to Satan, 'He is in your power; only spare his life.' So Satan went forth from the presence of the LORD and smote Job with severe boils from the soles of his feet to the crown of his head. And he took a potsherd to scrape himself, as he sat among the ashes. Then his wife said to him, 'Are you still holding to your innocence? Curse God and die.' But he said to her, 'Are even you going to speak as senseless women do? We accept good things from God; and should we not accept evil?' Through all this, Job said nothing sinful."* (Job 2:1-10)

Having obtained permission from God to test Job, Satan started with Job's material possessions, progressing from what Job possessed to what was his most intimate possession, that is, his own body. In all these trials the Lord had spared Job's life. These tribulations did not break Job down but, on the contrary, the trials strengthened Job's faith in God and his total dependence on God. Patiently enduring all these temptations only lifted Job to make him rise up completely renewed in a miraculous way: *"Also, the LORD restored the prosperity of Job, after he had prayed for his friends; the LORD even gave to Job twice as much as he had before. Then all his brethren and his sisters came to him, and all his former acquaintances, and they dined with him in his house. They grieved with him and comforted him for all the evil which the LORD had brought upon him; and each one gave him a piece of money and a gold ring. Thus the LORD blessed the latter days of Job more than his earlier ones. For he had fourteen thousand sheep, six thousand camels, a thousand yoke of oxen, and a thousand she-asses. And he had seven sons and three daughters, of whom he called the first Jemimah, the second Keziah, and the third Keren-happuch. In all the land no other women were as beautiful as the daughters of Job; and their father gave them an inheritance among their brethren. After this, Job lived a hundred and forty years; and he saw his children, his grandchildren, and even his great-grandchildren. Then Job died, old and full of years."* (Job 42:10-17)

In studying the Bible, we notice how God often puts his chosen ones to the test. St. James in his epistle says: *"My brothers, count it pure joy when you are involved in every sort of trial. Realize that when your faith is tested this makes for endurance. Let endurance come to its perfection so that you may be fully mature and lacking in nothing. If any of you is without wisdom, let him ask it from the God who gives generously and ungrudgingly to all, and it will be given to him. Yet he must ask in faith, never doubting, for the doubter is like the surf tossed and driven by the wind. A man of this sort, devious and erratic in all that he does, must not expect to receive anything from the Lord. Let the brother in humble circumstances take pride in his eminence and the rich man pride in his lowliness, for he will disappear 'like the flower of the field.' When the sun comes up with its scorching heat it parches the meadow, the field flowers droop, and with that the meadow's loveliness is gone. Just so will the rich man wither away amid his many projects. Happy the man who holds out to the end through trial! Once he has been proved, he will receive the crown of life the Lord has promised to those who love him. No one who is tempted is free to say, 'I am being tempted by God.' Surely God, who is beyond the grasp of evil, tempts no one."* (James 1:2-13) St. Paul writes: *"God keeps his promise. He will not let you be tested beyond your strength. Along with the test he will give you a way out of it so that you may be able to endure it."* (1 Cor. 10:13)

In conclusion, we infer that God sometimes allows the Evil One to act so that good may come from it. Then such temptations are not evil in themselves. Namely, God draws straight lines over the bent ones as much as man confides in God; He uses evil for our own good.

Obduracy in Sin

As an example of obduracy in Holy Scripture, we mention Judas, whose heart remained hardened to Jesus' repeated invitations and who was steeped in evil to the point of suicide. Specific obduracy in sin is visible in the sphere of sexual perversions, which are increasing more and more today, in different forms of violence, in alcoholism, drugs, deep-rooted hatred, unforgiveness and swearing. Extremely grave sins include abortion and adultery, to which we attribute the increasing incidences of divorce, thus causing enormous suffering for a number of people.

Sufferings Caused by Spells (Sorcery/Witchcraft)

With this type of satanic activity the victim is not to blame. However, the person who casts the spells and the one who commissions it commit a sin. This area is very slippery with the possibility for various kinds of deception, so much so that man has to be very prudent regarding potential fraud, deviations, suggestions and other similar nuances. Certainly there are ways to harm other people by casting spells on them through Satan's actions such as various charms, bindings, evil eyes, curses and so forth. It is difficult to understand that among priests, there are those who do not believe in spells. How effectively can they fight for their faithful who are being affected by this type of evil?

There are those who wonder how it is possible that God allows such evil. Man can use his freedom either for good or evil. He can help others or harm them, which he commonly does in an unjust or violent manner. For example, a man can pay a hit man to kill somebody. In like manner, he can pay a sorcerer or a witch to cast a spell on someone. Despite this, God is infinite Love and He wants salvation for everyone. In His goodness, He entices each one of us to love others, to forgive one another and to delight in the well-being of others. However, the Evil One does not remain quiet, for he puts into man's mind thoughts of revenge, judgment and hatred. What happens then? A man who does not pray and is not in the state of God's grace, or does not live in closeness to God, is left to his own devices, hardly able to oppose the Evil One on his own. Unfortunately, this man is overcome by the Evil One, and starts doing what God forbids. On the other hand, God does everything to encourage man to conversion.

It should be observed, however, that God respects man's decision in every situation since He created man as a free being and wants to abide by this principle of respecting man's free will until the end. God wants man to turn to Him out of his own free will. Therefore, we can say that God allows evil, but He never leaves man without sufficient aid by which he can oppose the Evil One with God's help.

Visiting Places or People who Practise Witchcraft

Here is a list of the most common and typical ways that evil activity is practised today: active participation or passive attendance at séances where spirits are invoked; engagement in different magical practices, whether black or white magic; visiting diviners, clairvoyants, pseudo-healers, sorcerers, radiesthesia practitioners (dowsers) and therapeutic touch practitioners (TTP), palm-readers, fortune-tellers, especially those who read tarot cards; diviners by coffee grounds, crystals, pendulum, dowsing rod; astrology and horoscope, and occult practitioners. We add to this participation in satanic sects or satanic rites that culminate in so-called black masses. Unfortunately, today all the means of communication are saturated with these offers and others of similar content.

Theatres, television and the internet offer pornography, horror, terror and violent films on a daily basis. Rock music is being propagated, reaching its peak in satanic rock, performed not only at stadiums and outdoor concert sites but also in disco bars. All of these and similar practices are increasing.

We can conclude that faith decreases in the same proportion with which these and similar magic practices increase. It is a serious but true statement that the majority of the clergy does nothing to stand up against these practices. It is necessary to speak about it in our churches with knowledgeable competence and educate our faithful about it, especially our young people who, ignorant and uninformed, rush headlong into satanic areas of activity, from which they can hardly escape. Satanic disturbances today are much more diffused among young people than in past decades.

Why Does God Allow the Activity of Evil Spirits?

Many people who come to ask for deliverance from their troubles ask me these or similar questions: Why does God allow this? Why does He allow the evil spirit to destroy my family? Why does God allow such tragedies in my family? Why this trial or that evil?

It is not possible to give a standard answer to these sorts of questions. There may be several reasons. We can divide them into three types:

- punishment for sin;
- God wants to prompt us to forgive;
- through these trials God wants us to become vigilant at all times, strong in our faith and in our trust in Him.

Punishment for Sin

It is not usual for man to plummet into sin suddenly. The most common way of falling is to start neglecting daily prayer which results in weakness and lukewarmness in one's religious life. This is usually followed by neglect in attending Sunday Mass, and in the observances of the Sacrament of Reconciliation and Holy Communion. Then other religious devotions are also neglected. So, when man starts to neglect and miss out on the means by which our faith is being fed and which God gives to the faithful through His Church, superstition begins to sneak into man in an unnoticeable and cunning manner. Namely, when man does not believe in the real God, he falls into a condition of religious indifference and starts to reject any form of religious observance. He becomes more engrossed in the spirit of rationalism that assures him that the human mind has a solution to every problem and that modern science is able to fix everything, so that he does not need God.

In rejecting God, who is an absolute Being, man elevates himself to the level of an absolute being, persuading himself that everything is possible for him. To put it simply, one turns oneself into God, and this idea in itself is at the core of atheism, whether man denies the existence of God, as in theoretical atheism, or lives and behaves as if God does not exist, and is not needed, as in practical atheism.

Here man inevitably falls into a kind of playacting, worshipping false gods or idols, pulled artfully by the Evil One. Man starts to worship money or material riches instead of God, and subjugates everything else in life according to this purpose. Some people become imprisoned by the lust for honor, excellence, or career progression and don't let anyone or anything stand in the way of accomplishing that goal. Other people have different idols like sports and rock stars, politicians, actors or other celebrity figures.

In rejecting God, man puts himself in God's place and thus allows for self-love and egoism to infiltrate his being. This perspective brings about various iniquities, fraud, gossip, calumnies, offenses, hatred, envy and jealousy, so that man sees his fellow man as an enemy, a threat to his life. This standpoint has an impact not only on human relationships but it carries also, in its nature, the root cause of endless political intrigues, criminal acts, a number of social injustices, exploitation of the majority of people for the benefit of enormously rich individuals who, unscrupulously, take advantage of others.

From this point of view, it is easy for man to lapse into absolute relativism in which nothing is sacred; everything is sanctioned in the name of corrupted freedom that, in its loftiness and arrogance, does not want to know of God's authority and His commandments. Such a view undermines every moral principle and, accordingly, everything is permitted. Various moral and religious delusions are spread, easily leading people into committing grave sins against the Holy Spirit, namely the sin of rejecting revealed truth.

Unfortunately, due to the spirit of this fallacious moral freedom, a certain overall confusion and insecurity is infiltrating the Church, to which theologians of different mindsets, quasi-theologians, with their ambiguous theories, confound simple Christian souls.

Today the most negative view of God has become, regretfully, the most expanded one in the form of Satanism. Satan wants to establish his kingdom more and more in our time; he has devised and planned it so that he may reign in the intelligence, memory, will, desires and actions of his followers. Sad to say, he continually wins over more devotees. If we keep all these facts in mind, then we will more readily understand why God allows those who have abandoned Him and left Him to become obsessed or possessed by the devil, for they themselves by their own free will have chosen the devil to be their 'god.' Only by going through a humiliating experience will they be able to receive a warning and be led to the right path. For many individuals, it is the way of gaining self-awareness and encountering the living God. This results in change and the conversion of hearts, so much so that large numbers of people have become truly convinced believers. Our people know about this and have a suitable proverb: "Every cloud has a silver lining!"

God Wants to Prompt Us to Forgive

In my long practice and in many cases where it was possible to establish beyond any doubt the influence of the Evil One, I discovered in conversations with people that Satan exerts a strong power over a person, even over whole families, because of their hatred and unforgivingness. My evaluation may seem too harsh, but I can testify from my own experience that there are rare cases where family members live in good and harmonious relationships among themselves and with other people. On the contrary, a number of people's relationships are disrupted and broken because of, for example, property disputes, usually among close relatives, like parents and children, or brothers and sisters, or a next-door neighbor.

In some cases, an offense or injustice done to an individual or to whole families may be the cause of an argument. The most common reasons may be obduracy in jealousy, envy or some kind of competition and rivalry, such as proving who is more influential or who has more power in society.

Satan is very skilled and knows well the nature of man which was impaired by original sin. He is able to perceive fragile and weak spots in one's character and is very adept at enticing man to awaken feelings of pride, obstinacy, hatred and revenge, consequently causing a long-term disruption in relations among individuals.

It is clear that where hatred, unforgivingness and stubbornness reign, there is no place for God, for God is love. In these circumstances man, even unconsciously, opens himself up to evil, therefore, to Satan. Satan takes control of the situation because people have created a space for him to manipulate. Only a few people really recognize that they are in the snare of the Evil One, and even they are not able to see how to free themselves from it.

When a man opens himself up to the Evil One and when the Evil One starts to take a hold over a man's life, it usually brings about immeasurable consequences in the lives of such persons and their families, which then afflict and trouble them, making them feel they are inside a vicious circle from which there is no way out.

In my encounters with people whose primary problem was hatred, even revenge, I always try to enlighten them that these problems arise and have their roots in unforgivingness, from which there is no way of deliverance or progress unless they reach the point of reconciliation.

To Peter's question: *"'Lord, when my brother wrongs me, how often must I forgive him? Seven times?' 'No,' Jesus replied, 'not seven times; I say, seventy times seven times.'"* (Mt. 18:21-22) Or, in other words, always.

Man is great in the act of forgiveness.

The first prerequisite for a man is to forgive in his heart. Then, with God's help, he can stretch his reconciling hand and simply forget, without turning back, whatever it is that separates him from another and causes an argument. Then it is necessary to reconstruct our relationships anew, based on love and mutual conciliation. Whenever this happens through God's grace, the Evil One has to back up and leave the premises in which he has been reigning for years, seducing people with his adept maneuvers. It usually happens that these people experience the mighty workings of God and a change in their lives, a fundamental conversion and new life in faith.

Alertness in Faith

Whenever we are idle in our faith or caught in spiritual feebleness, our sense of precaution diminishes so consequently, we open up space for the Evil One. He is always waiting for us. His ways of operating are manifested in the perversity by which he wishes to twist man's way of looking at things, so that evil then would be looked upon as good. We call this the devil's temptation, examples of which we find in the Gospels.

One time Jesus said these words to his apostles: *"Your faith in me will be shaken,"* (Mk. 14:27) which later they forgot. Obviously, if they had been watchful and had kept Jesus' warning in their mind, they wouldn't have fled when Jesus was captured. Without any doubt they would have stood by Jesus' side during His agony and death. The Gospels, on the contrary, report that: *"... all deserted him and fled."* (Mk. 14:50) Indeed, they left Jesus all alone.

Furthermore, Jesus also warned His disciples: *"I tell you solemnly, one of you will betray me."* (Jn. 13:21) Judas must have felt deep within himself that these words were meant for him. If he had kept watchful and strong in his faith, surely he wouldn't have betrayed his Master. In the Scriptures it is written: *"He dipped the morsel, then took it and gave it to Judas, son of Simon Iscariot. Immediately after, Satan entered his heart,"* (Jn. 13:26-27) and because he was not cautious, his faith had grown weary, so he lost the sense of moral judgment, turning Jesus over to the Jews for thirty pieces of silver.

The Gospels also reveal to us the moment, already mentioned, when Jesus warned His disciples: *"Your faith in me shall be shaken...,"* (Mk. 14:27) to which Peter replied: *"Even though all are shaken in faith, it will not be that way with me."* (Mk. 14:29) Jesus said to Peter *"I give you my assurance, this very night before the cock crows twice you will deny me three times."* (Mk. 14:30) All this came true when Jesus was tied up and brought into the high priest's palace, and Peter, who was standing in the courtyard with the servants fearing for his own life, disowned his Master three times with these words: *"I do not even know the man you are talking about."* (Mk. 14:71) If Peter had been on his guard and strong in his faith, he would not have fallen into this trap of sin and cowardly denial of Jesus after having being warned by his Master. After having learned from his own experience, Peter gave a warning to all of us in his epistle: *"Stay sober and alert. Your opponent the devil is prowling like a roaring lion looking for (someone) to devour. Resist him, solid in faith."* (1 Pt. 5:8)

Satan and his Snares

Satan 'Bestows' his Servants

There are those who abandon themselves to Satan, who then becomes their master. These people make a pact with Satan by willingly and completely surrendering to him. The pact is made up in a form of an imitation of the rite of baptism, which they sign with their own blood in the name of Satan. As a consequence, people fall under the complete and direct influence of Satan, their master. They perform black magic rituals in his name or become members of satanic sects which, sadly, are growing in number.

Satan 'bestows' his followers with very alluring but venomous gifts. Thus it can happen that some of his servants have powers of divination or of revealing one's past in detail. Some others receive messages and are able to write down many pages of text; others are endowed with gifts of clairvoyance, reading minds, hearts or lives, either of living or deceased people. In this way Satan is throwing mud at authentic prophets of Christ, genuine visionaries and receivers of messages from Jesus, Mary and the saints.

Satan can cause confusion by imitating God's work, which is the working of the Holy Spirit, so that people will not be able to discern who is or is not an authentic prophet. At this point, spiritual experience and the gift of discernment of spirits play a very important role, so that the discernment of authentic signs from the false ones can be made possible. There is a list of false signs in the book of Fr. Antonio Rogo Marin OP, "Theology of Christian Perfection" (the original title is: "Teologia della Perfezione Cristiana," Pubblicazione Paoline, page 1602), with the subtitle: "What the devil can do with God's permission." Here is the list of what the devil can do as related by the author:

1. cause physical and spiritual visual and auditory illusions;

2. cause a false state of ecstasy;

3. make a body radiate and cause a feeling of great warmth in the heart;

4. cause a sensual sweetness;

5. cure uncommon diseases in an instant that have originated from evil spirits;

6. cause stigmata and other sensory or mystical bodily occurrences, like pleasant odors and similar signs.

To this list we can add other manifestations that often occur in recent times: peculiar audio recordings, odd images captured by cameras (in cases when the photographs are not retouched), and automatic writing, usually related with so-called spiritual guidance. Among all of the saints, Satan and the occultists prefer to mystify by imitating St. Pio of Pietrelcina. People who are the most fanatically devoted to Padre Pio seek a way to receive the stigmata, become able to bilocate and so forth, all for the purpose of imitating him as truly as possible. When we see these types of signs occurring before our eyes, we are not looking at the work of God, but at the falsifications by which Satan wishes to pass off his impostors, imitators of Christ, Our Lady and the saints, as authentic charismatics.

For this reason the Church holds in higher regard evidence like holiness and a heroic living of evangelical virtues than the signs coming from a suspicious source. Therefore, we should not bow down before such a visible manifestation lest we bow down before 'God's ape,' who is doing everything to mock the mystery of Christ and His Precious Blood. The right way of discerning the nature of a manifestation and of a person directly involved with this dangerous occurrence is to send this person to a doctor, who will perform some tests and examine the case. In the same way this person should be directed to see and talk with an experienced exorcist who will then pray over him. Adequate discernment and evaluation is certainly called for in cases of religious pictures and statues that shed 'blood' or 'tears.'

In some circumstances and through the actions of false prophets, Satan testifies for the authenticity of true prophets of Christ, God's servants, so that people will reject them on account of such 'an acclaim.' A known incident is recorded in Acts when the apostle Paul went to stay in Thyatira. A slave woman, possessed by the evil spirit of divination, constantly followed Paul and with this ability, she brought a large profit to her owners. This possessed woman was shouting while following Paul and the others: *"These men are servants of the Most High God; they will make known to you a way of salvation."* (Acts 16:17) Surely the purpose of the soothsayer woman (or the evil spirit in her) and of her shouting after Paul was not to prompt people to seek salvation, but to reject Paul and the teachings of Christ because she, who was known to the public as possessed, was 'confirming' that Paul's mission was coming from God. Paul became so annoyed with all this that eventually he drove the demon out of her. (cf. Acts 16:16-18)

Let us recall that Holy Scripture offers not only similar examples of God's miraculous workings, but examples of Satan's miraculous workings as well. We are all familiar with the story of Moses who, in God's name, wrought miracles before Pharaoh. Those miracles are known as Egypt's plagues. It is also recorded that Egypt's sorcerers likewise wrought miracles. Therefore, the act of performing a miracle, if observed separately as an act in itself, is not sufficient for us to conclude as to what may be causing this miracle to occur. The truth is that an evil spirit always disguises himself very artfully with a purpose of remaining hidden: *"...And little wonder! For even Satan disguises himself as an angel of light."* (2 Cor. 11:14) With his actions Satan can stir up man's exterior senses: sight, touch, and hearing, as well as man's interior faculties: mind and imagination. There are no walls, or bullet-proof doors and bodyguards, that are able to prevent the influence of Satan on the mind or imagination of man. Even the sturdy fence of a strict Carmelite convent is not able to block Satan from jumping over the fence and inserting all sorts of images into the soul of a nun, causing her confusion regarding her vocation and, ultimately, enticing her to leave the religious community. For this reason there is a proverb saying that the most dangerous demon is 'the pious demon.' There is no place whatsoever where the devil is not able to sneak in, however holy it may be. In a particular way, he is known to present himself in sanctuaries, cloaked in pious clothing, where a large number of the faithful are gathered. The temptations that occur in such places are highly dangerous.

Satan Should be Properly Evaluated

Magic practices have been present throughout the whole history of mankind and in all nations. In our time, these practices are widely dispersed thanks to the mass media that advocate such practices so that many people have been ensnared in the devil's traps. On the other hand, many people, even the faithful, will just brush off and belittle any talk about satanic practices.

If we look at Holy Scripture, we will notice that it often speaks against magic and sorcerers in both the Old and the New Testaments. Here are some verses from the Bible: *"When you come into the land which the LORD, your God, is giving you, you shall not learn to imitate the abominations of the peoples there. Let there not be found among you*

51

anyone who immolates his son or daughter in the fire, nor a fortune-teller, soothsayer, charmer, diviner, or caster of spells, nor one who consults ghosts and spirits or seeks oracles from the dead. Anyone who does such things is an abomination to the LORD, and because of such abominations the LORD, your God, is driving these nations out of your way;" (Deut. 18:9-12) *"Do not go to mediums or consult fortune-tellers, for you will be defiled by them. I, the LORD, am your God;"* (Lv. 19:31) *"A man or a woman who acts as a medium or fortune-teller shall be put to death by stoning; they have no one but themselves to blame for their death;"* (Lv. 20:27) *"You shall not let a sorceress live."* (Ex. 22:17) In the New Testament, Jesus warns that we should be aware of the immense power of the devil. We should not challenge him but we should never stop fighting against him. Furthermore, Jesus gave us the power to cast out demons and taught us how to stand up against them because the devil is constantly firing bullets at us. And even Jesus Himself gave Satan permission to tempt Him in order to demonstrate to us how malicious, impertinent and persistent Satan is. Jesus gave us a clear warning that we cannot serve two masters and invited us to be alert always. We read the same admonishment in 1 Pt. 5:8-9: *"... Your opponent the devil is prowling like a roaring lion looking for (someone) to devour. Resist him, solid in faith..."*

Satan uses certain people whom he firmly binds to himself and who then, in turn, render him honor. Satan gives them the power to wield supernatural forces that are always destructive; in this way he recruits people for his service, turning them into slaves. Through the mediation of the evil spirit, these people can have negative and destructive effects on those who are separated from God in their daily activities. These persons are miserable and wretched. In fact, they have not learned about the meaning of life, suffering, troubles, pains or death and they long for happiness as it is presented in the world: well-being, riches, power, popularity and pleasure. And Satan continues tempting: *"He said to him, 'I will give you all this power and the glory of these kingdoms; the power has been given to me and I give it to whomever I wish. Prostrate yourself in homage before me, and it shall all be yours.'"* (Lk. 4:6-7)

And what happens? People of all kinds — young, old, common workers and intellectuals, men and women, politicians, actors, sports stars, curious people prompted by eagerness, as well as those who are burdened by personal or family troubles, psychological and physical problems — many of them often step into areas of magic and occult practices. Right there, waiting for them, are well-prepared and coordinated sorcerers, sorceresses, astrologists, soothsayers, clairvoyants, healers, prana therapists, therapeutic touch practitioners ('bioenergetics,' healing by using bio-energy), dowsers, hypnotists and many other psychic persons, in other words, the legion of masterly characters. People come to them for various reasons: some by chance, because everybody else does; curiosity; because they hold to a hope; others because they are desperate and in a dead-end situation. Many people think of these practices as fabrications, superstitions, frauds and inquisitiveness related only to the pursuit of a lucrative profit.

However, these domains of activity are not as guileless or innocent as they may seem. Magic is not just an idle chanting without any foundation in reality. On the contrary, it is a highly dangerous area where magicians of all kinds turn to demonic forces so that by subjecting themselves to them, they can affect the flow of events and people's lives, while procuring for themselves some earthly benefit. The objectives of these practices are always the same: to distance man from God, entice him to sin and, lastly, to prepare the foundations for man's eternal death.

We should not underestimate the power of Satan. He is a cunning liar who always wishes to drag us off towards false beliefs and extremism. If he cannot convince us of his non-existence or if he fails to entrap us into one of his concrete devices, then he will endeavor to make us believe in his omnipresence and dominion over everything. He takes advantage of man's feeble faith and weakness to instill fear in him. He wants to shatter man's faith in the mighty power, love and mercy of God. Thus, it happens that some people see evil everywhere and talk about it all the time. This notion may also be classified as one of the devil's traps, for a mere look from God is stronger than any evil whatsoever and just one drop of His Blood can save the whole world.

The Origin of Satan's Presence in the Life of an Individual

When a person having serious problems calls on a priest for help, the priest should, with God's grace, try to discern the key problem and what the origin of this problem is. It is necessary to see from where and in what manner evil entered the life of the individual concerned. It is essential to distinguish these particulars concerning each unique situation so that a person involved could be set free and step away from the concrete, malicious maelstrom.

From my long personal practice, through my readings on the subject and cooperation with those involved in this field, I have realized that there are more sources and ways in which evil can enter into the life of a man.

The main problem that tortures a person, which may transform and multiply into many problems later on, has its origins in:

- the family tree
- emotional (spiritual) wounds
- personal sins
- satanic practices

It is essential to know that these four areas have an inter-connective pattern of cause and effect, overlapping in their influence in the life of a person. Having a problem in one area of life facilitates the penetration of evil in another area of life.

The Family Tree

It is beyond doubt that each person is individually responsible before God for his own deeds. Many biblical messages clearly reveal this. On the other hand, the Bible brings us the following verses as well: *"The Lord, the Lord, a merciful and gracious God, slow to anger and rich in kindness and fidelity, continuing his kindness for a thousand genera-*

tions, and forgiving wickedness and crime and sin; yet not declaring the guilty guiltless, but punishing children and grandchildren to the third and fourth generation for their father's wickedness!" (Ex. 34:6–7) That is, if our ancestors — fathers, grandfathers or great-grandfathers — did evil in their lives, the condemnation passes on to their descendants in a particular manner for we are all spiritually connected, like shackles in a chain: the stronger the blood bond, the stronger the effect it produces. Just as various physical diseases are hereditary, in a similar manner the spiritual inclinations are being transmitted as well. If our forefathers did not repent of their sins, it can be manifested as a substantially heavy burden on posterior generations. It is especially distressful if a murder or suicide occurred in a family; a sudden death, if a family member was a member of some criminal or ideological party (fascist or communist); if the burial place of an ancestor is unknown; if bizarre events took place in their lives such as the horrible death of little children; if an ancestor dedicated his life to God and then broke his vows or turned his back on the Church; if an ancestor committed adultery, fornicated or had a deliberate abortion; if there were serious thefts or a gambling problem, addiction to alcohol, drugs, etc. The effects of the sin of hatred and unforgiveness can permeate deeply on the descendants. People who were involved in these evil activities and did not repent, not only burdened themselves, but also left a distressing and oppressive legacy to their descendants which weighs on them so much that they can hardly remove it. It is very important to mention cases in which ancestors participated in magic and occult, whereby their descendants intensely feel the working of Satan in their lives.

We should know that a spiritual legacy exists and that we inherit it from our ancestors at the very moment of our conception. This is the reason why it is especially important to make peace with God so that we save our souls and do not become an obstacle for peace in the lives of our descendents.

We ought to forgive our ancestors, pray for them often with all our heart, actively using all the means of salvation that Mother Church offers us.

Emotional (Spiritual) Wounds

The fundamental problem in the life of a person who comes to see a priest may lie in some past emotional wound. We experience traumas from the very moment of our conception and later on, they have a strong negative effect on our whole lives. When traumas occur up to the third or fourth year of a life, they are particularly distressing and become deeply suppressed. Our spirit is the same at the moment of our conception to the present time; the spirit sees and knows while the soul feels all the pain inflicted on it. In the prenatal stage of life and in early childhood, we are unable to give rational explanations about what is happening to us, just as we are powerless to defend ourselves.

In these early tender years of life, when a person experiences a serious trauma, his soul is injured. The child's soul is wounded by sin that is not his but that of the person who hurt him. From that moment on the child becomes emotionally ill. The feelings that dominate the person who has suffered a serious emotional wound usually are: rejection, guilt, a feeling of inferiority or fear. These are the most common fundamental problems that generate new and concrete troubles even on the physical level. Many psychosomatic ailments may have their origin in this primary emotional wound, as well as asthma, allergies and migraines.

At first glance it could be said that emotional wounds do not have their origin in the influence of the Evil One. This, however, is not correct; they do. The primary wound originates as a consequence of an evil act inflicted by another person upon the victim, and Satan is always the one who tempts the perpetrator to sin. Thus, when we are dealing with a person whose fundamental problem is an emotional wound, while we pray for the emotional healing of that person, we should also pray for the spiritual deliverance and the grace of God's forgiveness for the person who inflicted the hurt. We should likewise pray for grace so that the injured person can forgive those who were responsible for the wound.

Spiritual or emotional wounds are always deeper if the person who inflicted them is a close relative (father, mother, brother. . .). It happens frequently that when we pray for the mother, her child gets cured, or in order for a mother to be healed, we have to pray for the healing and deliverance of the mother's father or even husband, or other relative.

A person can become emotionally wounded in later periods of his life. These wounds could be very serious, but they are not usually as deeply repressed into the subconscious as happens in the case when they are inflicted in the early period of life. These wounds may also be caused by another person's sin (e.g., rape, witnessing to a grave crime.). In such cases, the victim could be held responsible only if he had committed the sin of omission or imprudence.

The basic problem for people suffering from emotional wounds is that they usually engage themselves in many occult practices before turning to a priest for assistance, whereby the whole problem becomes only more difficult. In such cases Satan can be both the primary cause of their problem as well as a hindrance for discovering and healing the source of all their difficulties. The spirits of hatred and unforgiveness often assault individuals suffering from serious emotional wounds, possessing them in such a way as to destroy their lives and make them trespass gravely against themselves and others.

The emotional healing and deliverance of these persons occurs when they truly decide to turn to God and sincerely and utterly forgive those who have hurt them. It is worth saying that psychiatry and medicine obtain little effect in these cases. This is an area in their lives where Satan exerts his influence over them mostly through the sin of another person. Such situations and all the things involved with them ought to be surrendered to Jesus so that through Him they can start to love themselves and those who have hurt them.

Personal Sins

The most common reason for Satan's influence on man's life is man's personal sin. It consists of the conscious and voluntary decision of an individual to act against God. Personal sins differ in gravity and can be committed in thoughts, words, deeds and omission. The gravest sins are deeds because a deed is always a completed act. However, it should be said that only God knows the actual seriousness of every personal sin.

When we speak of a sin as a cause for the Devil's presence in man's life, we clearly speak of a personal sin as a decision against God and in favor of Satan. Thus, at the moment when a man consents to sin, he chooses Satan, at which point the Evil One enters his life and to a certain extent exerts power over him. This type of sin can be so destructive that only later may a person discover how this particular sin was the fundamental cause of all his problems. Whoever keeps on committing a specific sin is likely to suffer from a lethal and vicious virus of the Evil One, and consequently will give in more often to temptation. Since sin is a sickness of the spirit, it progresses and metastasizes up to a point of affecting the soul and body.

Taking into consideration the topic of this book, we will now give special attention to the sins against the first commandment of God, the sins of idolatry. We know that breaking God's first commandment includes breaking ultimately all of God's commandments. Satan knows this too. He knows that if he manages to persuade a man to say 'NO' to God and choose him instead, he has more or less succeeded in everything else. Namely, the Evil One is the father of lies, the accuser of his fellow creatures and a murderer from the beginning. Obviously, there is little doubt about where the life of a man who has bowed to Satan is heading. That is why Satan does all he can to entice a man to trespass against the first commandment and in order to do it, he will even disguise himself as an angel of light. (cf. 2 Cor. 11:14)

In our century man lives in surroundings where every authority has renounced God or has overtly turned against Him or, alternatively, in surroundings where there is no authority or responsibility at all and where everything is allowed. Unfortunately, these two evils complement each other perfectly.

Young people today are often seduced by the sins of sexuality; they are persuaded that premarital intercourse is something natural and that masturbation brings relief to a person, channelling one's energy and tension. So much evil is spread among young people with the help of indecent magazines. Unfortunately, parents often bring these kinds of magazines into the home, causing the ruin of their own children. The young are being persuaded that the consumption of alcohol and drugs will release them from anguish and trauma. The Evil One is being offered to them through the practices of magic and various occult activities. They get involved more or less consciously in such practices, committing the grave sin of idolatry. After some time, when their problems become more difficult, they ask for help from pseudo-healers or join different sects instead of turning to God and to the ministers of the Church. There is a saying that evil begets evil. And we well know that Satan cannot drive Satan away.

Every sin has to be deeply repented, especially a sin that is the fundamental cause of all other problems manifesting themselves later on in the life of an individual. One should confess, renounce the sin, atone for having offended God and then have recourse to God's immense mercy. This is the only way in which man can liberate himself from the satanic influence that entered his life through personal sin. The most dangerous and extremely detrimental thing is to persist in sinning, to want to sin, hence turning particular sin or sins into abominable gods. One ought to crush all idols and put the real Triune God in first place. It is He who has revealed himself to us in Jesus Christ, our Lord.

Satanic Practices

This area includes a very wide range of activities, about which much has been written without having been studied fully. Since the Evil One tends to disguise and entangle everything, it is sometimes very difficult to differentiate one thing from another or decide what belongs where in relation to his activity. The servants of Satan are often active in diverse occult practices. They wrap themselves in allegedly scientifically verifiable formulae, then finally envelop the servant-slaves one more time in a cocoon of malevolent kindness.

Occultism and Magic

In this chapter I wish to touch upon a vast area of activity where Satan is reaping an abundant harvest, especially in our times.

The word 'occultism' derives from the Latin word 'occultus' which means hidden, secret and dark. Thus occultism would be an attempt to enter the mysterious, dark world of unknown forces. In fact, this mysterious world is made up of those phenomena in nature whose occult causes cannot be scientifically proven. People who are working in the scientific fields avoid the term occultism and prefer the concept of parapsychological phenomena that are dealt with using parapsychology. These are the phenomena in nature whose origin cannot be explained by the natural laws known at the present.

Man has always shown interest in the domain of the occult, i.e. the mysterious. In particular, man has always wanted to peek behind the curtain covering the future of his life. To achieve this goal he has resorted to various occult and magic practices such as divination by the examination of coffee grounds, palm reading, cards (specifically tarot cards); the inquisitive perusal of the horoscope in daily newspapers; reading of astrological magazines and numerous kinds of literature related to occultism and magic; consulting dream books; using the pendulum (radiesthesia); and invoking spirits (spiritism). Unfortunately and with great concern we have to acknowledge that even youth and children today accept and practise more and more witchcraft as well as dabble in magical formulas, exotic cult procedures, astrology, ji-jing, yoga, transcendental meditation, Zen Buddhism, judo, karate, Kabbalah, acupuncture, chiropractic, reiki, paragnosis, psychometry and psychoscopy, chiromancy, cartomancy, crystallomancy, astromancy, rhabdomancy, irimancy and other types of magical practices. Moreover, for the sake of popularity many people enter different sects like Hare Krishna, followers of Sai–Baba, Maharishi, Jehovah's Witnesses, Quakers, Mormons (the Church of Jesus Christ of Latter-day Saints), Seventh Day Adventists, New Apostolic Church, Christian Science (Scientology), Baha'i, Assembly of Christ Church, Pentecostalism and so forth. Satanic sects are especially notorious for their morbidity and powerful demonic activity.

Young people are increasingly enthusiastic about the New Age, which has diffused widely and in an organized manner trying to create a New World Order which is, in fact, Satan's clever potion of Christianity and previously-mentioned sects. Under this guise, it operates in a concrete manner in all areas of human life upon which a man depends (the area of culture, education, medicine, economy, politics, etc.) due to their nature.

A great number of books and periodicals dealing with occult practices are being published with a vast circulation. Some are even published in secret. These books teach and direct people how to become engaged in the ominous world of occultism and magic. Statistics show that twenty million Europeans frequently take part in occult activities. In Germany there are more than three million adherents of occultism together with another five to ten million sympathizers of occult teachings. The figures from the United States set the number of Americans who practice sorcery and magic at ten million, among whom are many highly-educated people. Therefore, the engagement in the occult and magic is not reserved only for so-called 'primitive people' but in great measure it is also practised throughout the circles of higher western culture.

Now, it should be quite clear that under the term of magic we do not refer to what is being performed on stage by illusionists (magicians – 'hocus-pocus'), all dressed in fine clothes, pulling white rabbits from black top-hats. In other words, it is not the matter of having dextrous fingers but concerns paranormal powers that always have their source in the operation of the occult and devilish forces, behind which there is none other than Satan himself.

Some people become involved in magical practices out of curiosity, while for others it is a fashionable thing to do. A number of people will say that they do not take these practices seriously and will reason that it cannot do them any harm whatsoever. But Satan takes these 'occult games' very seriously. And again, many times we have to see and be convinced that sooner or later Satan will grasp every hand stretched out to him in his iron clench, not letting it go very easily. For he who plays with fire will get burned and it is unimportant whether one believes in the destructive force of the fire.

Using these and similar practices, a man opens the door to the evil forces and blindly exposes himself to the negative forces of the Evil One, consciously or unconsciously, whereby all kinds of problems spring up, accompanied often by heavy disorders on both mental and physical levels. When this starts to happen, people begin to complain about being haunted by a feeling of fear; or they become strangely introverted and shun others; or they feel a deep hatred and inability to forgive another; or they become rather distracted, especially in prayer; they are doubtful, distrustful, vengeful, and feel anguish; they experience acute and unbearable tensions in their family; they have compulsive thoughts of suicide; they sense an unwillingness and aimlessness; they feel constant restlessness and are tormented with nightmares. Others begin to hear obsessive voices inside themselves; others feel they are being forced to do certain acts which they do not want to do. Many sense emotional and at times even physical disturbances; some people cannot be freed from a certain vice, some think they possess a healing energy or talk to the spirits and hallucinate about receiving unusual revelations from other worlds, etc. Unfortunately, people experience all of this without knowing what is going on at all. These are just some of the indications that undoubtedly point to the negative influence of the evil spirits on man.

Regarding baptized persons, the negative influence is vastly manifested in a continuous disruption of their communication with God. Difficulties arise in prayer and in reading Holy Scripture; there is a stoppage, a distinctive barrier to their spiritual growth. They brood on gloomy doubts about salvation; have blasphemous thoughts; lack spiritual discernment; have a diminished sense of faith and joy and a growing lack of interest in Jesus Christ and his Gospel; they experience a detachment from Him.

Persons involved in the occult and magical practices very frequently have problems in moral and mental areas of their lives: they tend to become depressed, aggressive, feel as if they have been imprisoned, and, in the sexual field, experience different types of perversities, deviations and also some kind of unnaturally compulsive sexual activity.

When people find themselves in evil surroundings, it is normal for them to start asking for assistance. However, it is very interesting to find that, as if by some rule, people often go to the wrong places, mostly seeking out witches, fortune-tellers, clairvoyants, pseudo-healers, astrologists, therapeutic touch healers, and dowsers. All of these are involved in magical practices, in other words, in Satan's business. These persons are often apt to protect themselves by placing holy pictures and statues in their homes so as to convince the ignorant faithful of how their work is aligned with the power of God, which just serves as a smokescreen to hide their magic schemes. I will illustrate this with one example from my experience.

I happened to see a business card from a pseudo-healer. On one side of her card was a picture of the Holy Trinity, figures of the Father, the Son and the Holy Spirit, with a text beside it: "Glory be to the Father and the Son, and the Holy Spirit." The other side read: "Healing hands (distance healing), removal of spells and divination (by tarot cards)," then it showed her name, her phone numbers (she had three phone numbers in one town and three more in another town), and, finally, her cellphone number. In fact it was a well-expanded business. The person who gave me this card had visited this healer and told me of the high prices she charged for her services. Indeed, what a way to fool people!

All the mass media — newspapers, certain radio and TV programs, among others — are overflowing with flattering offers and attractive commercials coming from the areas of magic and the occult. Regrettably, many people seek solutions for their troubles and living circumstances on the dark side of the bank. Despite the example above, we know that Satan cannot expel himself. (cf. Mk. 3:23-27) Therefore, a person seeking help from the other side can only worsen his/her lot. Not only does one not receive deliverance from evil but one can only cement oneself much deeper with these practices. Many people have personally experienced this.

Black Magic or Witchcraft

This sinister practice of invoking Satan aims to direct satanic evil against a person by employing magic formulas and rites that are always mysterious and are sometimes intertwined in their nature. To be able to exert influence on a person, a sorcerer asks for a person's personal belongings: hair, nail clippings, skin, a piece of underwear, a photograph …Then he suggests to his victim rules of procedure that must be observed in a strict manner for a successful outcome. For example: a person has to visit seven churches, light a candle in a specific manner, scatter ashes, go to the cemetery and place objects on a grave or take away some objects from a grave, or a person has to wear objects for 'protection', put them in certain places, consume certain food or potions.

I have assisted distressed and frightened mothers many times because they took their children to sorcerers and received from them certain objects to put on their children. At first this may seem naïve and insignificant but in time this practice reveals its malicious effects because it is truly satanic.

Magic astrology is a known practice of preparing various magical objects by sorcerers: pentacles, charms and talismans. And when some people go through certain evil situations such as: accidents, family misunderstandings, suffering from poverty or lack of love, are stricken and haunted by fears and phobias, they feel happy if they can receive those objects for 'protection' from certain sorcerers and are convinced that such objects will deliver them from their troubles. On top of all this, people are glad to pay high prices to obtain objects that will bring them 'luck.' However, using and carrying these objects creates a highly-negative energy that brings great harm not only to those who receive them but often to all members of a family in whose homes such objects can be found.

Magic potions are also used in magic. These potions cause suggestions or diabolic harassment to a person who swallows them because sorcerers invoke sinister spirits while they prepare them. A potion is then secretly mixed with food or drink. One such well-known potion is the so-called 'love potion' that can create a terrible bond through the mediation of satanic forces.

With sorcery, it is a characteristic that an individual comes personally and seeks 'help' from a sorcerer and the sorcerer then advises this person that only by performing some actions and employing certain objects will the person achieve a goal.

At this point I would like to emphasize some specifics. If one steps into the territory of the enemy and his circle, one puts oneself under the enemy's influence and control, despite the fact of naiveté, ignorance and lack of malice in doing so. In such cases Satan has a kind of joint ownership over this person and will not abandon him easily. In this way, man has been exposed to the forces of evil and has entered Satan's vicious circle from which only the hand of the Almighty God can deliver him. For the Evil One is stronger than man. In such situations, man is completely helpless as if guided by some force he cannot fight. However, God is immensely stronger than the Evil One. That is why God is the only way to deliverance and salvation.

Spells (Hexes) or Spell Casting

There is a classic definition that says that spell casting is "the art of doing harm to other persons with the help of the devil." Today we are overwhelmed with people who are engaged in these negative activities. To this circle of spell casters we can add various types of cartomancers, palm readers, sorcerers, and witches, sects of black magic, satanic sects, necromancers, fortune tellers and all kinds of people who, in one way or another, have something in common with satanic workings. Both the Old Testament and the New Testament give strict condemnations of such practices: *"Do not practise divination or soothsaying;"* (Lv. 19:26) *"Do not go to mediums or consult fortune-tellers, for you will be defiled by them;"* (Lv. 19:31) *"A man or a woman who acts as a medium or fortune-teller shall be put to death by stoning; they have no one but themselves to blame for their death;"* (Lv. 20:27) *"When you come into the land which the LORD, your God, is giving you, you shall not learn to imitate the abominations of the peoples there. Let there not be found among you anyone who immolates his son or daughter in the fire, nor a fortune-teller, soothsayer, charmer, diviner, or caster of spells, nor one who consults ghosts and spirits or seeks oracles from the dead. Anyone who does such things is an abomination to the LORD, and because of such abominations the LORD, your God, is driving these nations out of your way. You, however, must be altogether sincere toward the LORD, your God. Though these nations whom you are to dispossess listen to their soothsayers and fortune-tellers, the LORD, your God, will not permit you to do so."* (Deut. 18:9-14)

The usual way of harming another person is by offering certain objects to Satan, who then imprints on those his malevolent force. Here a specific material is used with the specific purpose of harming others. It is significant to observe how Satan often imitates God. Namely, every sacrament has a particular material that is used. For example, a substance like water (for baptism). The same happens when a spell is being cast, only Satan uses the material with a malicious purpose of hurting people.

Real and authentic spells and hexes are out there. They are conjured up by individuals who have made a pact with Satan, and through this action an evil spirit inflicts harm on others. These persons live on hatred, envy and cunning, just like the evil spirits do. That is crucial to emphasize because many people today, even priests, do not believe in the existence of hexes.

I would like to give an account of a true case. Marina (not her real name) had been having severe nausea for three years but only at nighttime. Whenever she entered the bedroom she would start to breathe heavily, choke, become very restless; she would also get a strong urge to vomit, experience excruciating headaches, and then finally she would faint. Her mother would call 911, but as soon as they arrived at the hospital the symptoms would stop. The doctors would ascertain then that she was in perfect health. When she came back home, everything would start all over again at the moment she entered her bedroom, and in particular when she laid down on the pillow. She would start to feel great pains all over her body that it made it impossible for her to fall asleep. She visited several different specialists who undertook on more than one occasion all the necessary check-ups and concluded that her illness might be connected to epileptic seizures. However, the brain scans did not verify the doctors' suspicions.

One day a family friend suggested that Marina go to an exorcist. After the first three prayers of exorcism and the blessing of their house nothing improved and the attacks kept recurring. The exorcist advised Marina to live as faithfully as possible her Christian life and to keep sprinkling her house with the blessed water. Furthermore, the exorcist advised that all the pillows in the house should be shredded. He suspected that the hex was hidden in Marina's pillow. He gave this advice to everyone in the house for he thought if he had singled out Marina she might have felt uncomfortable. Nothing was discovered in any of the pillows except Marina's pillow where a piece of burial linen was found. The piece was long and wide matching the size of the pillow, and had many feathers in the form of a funeral wreath pinned to it. The exorcist advised Marina to sprinkle it with the blessed water and then burn it. Only after she had followed the advice completely did the nausea stop and she was finally restored to sound sleep. Marina is now doing fine and has taken up everyday duties again. She feels rested and lives a true Christian life, and her family lives in serenity after many temptations. The main purpose of the enchanted black linen in Marina's pillow was meant to gradually drive Marina crazy and lead her to despondency so that she would ultimately end her life. It was further discovered that a family in the neighborhood ordered the spell out of pure hatred and envy. Even though they wished to bring about the death of the entire family, Marina turned out to be the only victim in all this horror.

Demonic activity can also target man's material surroundings, in particular through objects and places, with a single purpose of exerting an influence on man. Frequent targets of such an influence are houses, furniture, lamps and various items in use that are consequently being destroyed. It can happen that noises and banging are heard without any source whatsoever. Working appliances that run perfectly suddenly stop functioning properly or become damaged. Objects catch fire suddenly, or black stains start to appear on walls. Places without water installations get flooded. Many other inexplicable things can happen, such as lucrative businesses collapsing, livestock dying, whole crops getting ruined or fields being destroyed by an invasion of insects. When experts come across such occurrences they are helpless. The occurrence disappears only after the prayer of exorcism is prayed, or after sacramentals like blessed water and exorcised salt have been used.

Poisoning Spells

This can happen in cases when a person or the victim takes food or drinks concoctions mixed with charms. Spells can be made from various ingredients: bones of corpses; menstrual blood; different powders (the most frequently used are black, burnt parts of animals, especially the heart); also some special herbs and similar materials. The effect of a hex does not depend much on the material that has been employed but more on the intention and the hatred of the person who wishes to harm another through Satan's evildoings. There are a number of secret formulas that sorcerers utter while they prepare vile concoctions. That is the reason why a person, targeted as the recipient, begins to experience different disturbances. The most characteristic one is aches and pains in the stomach, from which one can be set free only through prayer that is usually accompanied with profuse vomiting of the strangest mixture.

Love Spells

Love spells are intended to accomplish one of two goals, either to make one person hate another or to make one person fall in love with another. It all depends on the intention of the perpetrator. One way which this is achieved is to imbue with malice the objects which belong to the victim, like photos, pieces of clothing, any of the person's personal belongings. It is also possible to infuse with malice effigies like dogs, puppets and even living persons of the same age and sex that may represent the victim. The procedure employed in this case consists of performing specific evil actions on a medium. The performed actions are sufferings that one wishes to inflict on another. For instance, during one such satanic ritual, pins were stuck in the head of a doll that represented the recipient of the attack. It often happens that the victim begins to have headaches. Also, other sharp items like needles, knives and nails are pierced through the various parts of a doll that represents the person against whom the evil is intended. The unfortunate victim starts to feel pains all over the body, in the exact spots where the doll is pierced. The deliverance takes place only after the prayer of the Church is prayed and the pins and nails have been removed from the doll, thereby putting an end to this satanic ritual.

Spells of Decay

This is the spell of killing. The procedure is performed by burying a charmed item in the ground of the victim's house. At the same rate that this item is slowly disintegrating into dust, the victim is developing an illness. This spell results in an overall psychosomatic exhaustion which slowly but surely leads to death. Neither a general practitioner nor a specialist can find the cause of illness. The most modern medical diagnostic equipment cannot determine the cause of the illness of this patient. On the contrary, the results of medical analyses usually show that the person is in perfect health, while the patient simply continues to fade and finally dies. This form of spell is, beyond any doubt, one of the most horrible spells that is becoming, regretfully, more and more common.

In addition to this, there are spells of tying the bonds in order to harm a baby in the mother's womb. They are conjured up by tying with hair or colored ribbons the parts of a doll that represent the child in the mother's womb, the victim of the spell. The goal is to affect the specific parts of the child's body, thus causing disfigurement of the body after birth or putting a barrier to its regular development. The spell is often focused on the child's mental development and growth that can later result in disturbances during the child's studies, duties and normal behavior.

The spells are cast through various unusual objects found in pillows and mattresses, such as pieces of wood, iron, blood clots, densely-tangled woman's hair or child's hair, colored and knotted ribbons, ropes full of knots and similar items. Sometimes these objects are not visible at first when the mattresses and pillows are torn but when blessed water is sprinkled or sometimes when a picture of Our Lady is put on those objects, or a cross, the most extraordinary objects appear.

Spells of Transfer

The evil influence of the spell can sometimes be cast against married couples, engaged couples and even against a friend in order to ruin them. During my pastoral practice I have seen cases where engaged couples really loved and desired each other very much but they were not able to maintain their relationship and had to break up unexpectedly and for no reason whatsoever. On one occasion, a girl fell in love with her best friend's fiancé. In order to win his love and achieve her goal to make her plan come to fruition through magic, she visited a sorcerer who was dealing with charms and spells. This marriage was a terrible marriage. Even though they could never fully accept each other, the husband was unable to leave his wife. They lived together truly in hell.

At times marriages are formed without love and against the will of the engaged parties just because it was the will of the parents or other persons who ordered spell casting that would make a victim act against his/her own will. People come to their senses only when their problems are overwhelming. They make a hell of their lives which can only be redeemed through the Blood of Christ. Sometimes a victim of spell casting is not aware of the existence of a spell and at other times is deceived and brought before a sorcerer. It is evident that the victim has no problem and does not ask for the sorcerer's assistance himself, but another person, driven by malice and rancor, visits the sorcerer so he can bewitch the despised victim with various charms. Often individuals who wish to hurt another are also themselves engaged in spell casting and incantation, pushed by hatred from within.

When people are inflicted by magical workings and bear the heavy consequences of it, they seek to pull themselves out of trouble. Satan then leads them, as if by some rule, to sorcerers, his servants, who beguile people by telling them how their activity specifically involves white magic that can remove the spells according to them. Sorcerers thus extort money from wounded people, dragging them into greater evil. With their satanic practices they may obtain temporary healing for a patient. However, their evil then passes onto their spouse, children, parents or siblings, which is often manifested in a form of inveterate lapse of faith, obduracy in sin, frequent car accidents, depression, fears, suicides and the like.

What should one do with magical objects either found or received?

All such objects must be sprinkled with blessed water and burned, not in the house but somewhere outside and in the open. Ashes, iron items and other objects that cannot be burned, after having been passed through flames, should be thrown in a place where water flows, in a stream, river, the sea or into a garbage container that is disposed of in an incinerator. It is not advisable to flush such objects down one's toilet as the sewage system can get clogged and the house may be flooded. During the process of destroying magical objects in fire, it is important to pray and invoke the protection of the most Precious Blood of Jesus, and then wash one's hands with holy water.

It is worth pointing out here that it is quite common to encounter in many cities 'deeply pious individuals,' men and women, whom we 'see regularly in church' and who are believed to have the ability to break spells, remove charms or ward off an evil eye. Such persons will give a victim of enchantment a medal or a cross, or another item like 'little red horns' or 'the wolf's teeth,' or some sort of small bundles and then advise them to carry these items for protection. The objects mentioned are not charged with the negative energy through a magical rite that sorcerers regularly perform but are connected, nevertheless, with Satan through the sin of superstition. Such objects should be burned as well. And one should call on a priest for assistance instead of turning to these 'pious individuals.'

Spiritism (Invocation of the Spirits)

Undoubtedly, Spiritism is one of the most dangerous magical practices. In fact, this is an attempt to enter into communication with the spirits of the departed or with higher spirits. It is performed by calling upon hidden forces that never come from God, but from hell. Spiritism is a means of spreading the kingdom of the Prince of Darkness on earth. Therefore individuals who abandon themselves to spiritism join a church of Satan. This practice is known in all cultures and nations. In spiritism there is always a person, i.e. a medium, who is the mediator between the spirits and people. The medium offers his voice, movements, writing ... to the spirit that is asked to manifest itself. Such spirits are always demons! Therefore, it can happen that one of the persons present at a séance becomes possessed. The Church has always condemned spiritistic séances, participation in and even the mere attendance at séances as well. One can never learn anything good by asking Satan for advice.

This sort of practice, as well as all that is mysterious and the occult, attracts man and arouses his curiosity. Primary school children, high school children and often adults fall into the temptation of spiritism. I am familiar with one group of highly-educated university graduates and intellectuals who regularly hold séances.

In my long years of experience, I have come to the firm conclusion that all those who are engaged in practising spiritism, as if by a rule, become assaulted by dark and suicidal thoughts. Sooner or later and during some trial period in their lives, they meditate on suicide, which many of them eventually commit. Satan gloats the most when he strips all those who approach him and his devilish circle of the meaning of life, dragging them to the edge from where they are unable to see the way out. In such an extreme state of depression, man can easily take his own life. The recently-increased rate of suicidal incidents in our country may be attributed to spiritistic and other magical and occult practices. Their manifestations and consequences are visible in psychophysical deterioration, moral and religious decadence, insomnia, irritation, heavy nightmares and phobias.

At times it happens that an evil spirit abides in a certain place where the invocation of spirits has taken place and that evil keeps obsessing every one of those who were present at the séance. When a victim wants to go to sleep and turns the lights off, the evil spirit comes and harasses the victim, making him go insane.

Many questions arise: Is it possible to invoke the spirits? Are the spirits that appear at séances always evil spirits? People ask these questions bearing in mind the account described in the Bible in which Saul, the king of Israel, turned to a witch and commanded her: *"Tell my fortune through a ghost; conjure up for me the one I ask you to."* (1 Sam. 28:8) In fact, Samuel the prophet who had passed away some time before, appeared. Obviously, God allowed this exception to happen. The most important fact to note is the frightened scream of the medium as well as Samuel's sharp rebuff: *"Why do you disturb me by conjuring me up?"* (1 Sam. 28:15) We must respect the departed and not disturb them. This is the only example of conjuring up a departed soul that is described in the Bible and I refer to it as an exception. Our beloved departed ones need our prayers to free them from the purifying pains. This is the only thing we can do for them. It is most certain that God doesn't allow departed souls to be used for our earthly plans whatsoever.

At this point I would like to exhort my colleagues in the priesthood to open their eyes to the situation in which we live which is impregnated with all forms of Satanism. People around us are simply suffocating in evil and it seems as if we are blind to this fact because we remain mostly immobile and uninterested. In the meantime, malignant spirits relentlessly continue with their work, focusing on their ultimate and sole intent to separate victims from God, enticing them to sin and causing them anguish, depression, alienation and despair. Through the investment in the Sacrament of Holy Orders and with Christ's power, a priest is the only person who is called and authorized to combat and overcome evil effectively, to liberate souls from Satan's influence. The faithful are entitled to anticipate such a ministry from us. If we fail to embrace and understand them, if we do not find the time to help them, we will bear an enormous responsibility before God for their waywardness. If people are weighed down by the evil that is always stronger than man, then they look for help in all directions. Mostly they turn to sorcerers, various pseudo-healers, clairvoyants and similar characters who, through magic, which is one of the satanic practices, do not deliver people but pull them more tightly into the vicious circle from where they do not see a way out. Unfortunately, I regularly come across these and other sorts of cases in my practice.

Cursing

Cursing is one of the most dangerous ways to harm another person. Whoever is cursing or maledicting wants to inflict an evil on another, and we all know that the source of evil is Satan. If the curse is uttered with true venom, in particular if the curser and the accursed are blood related, the consequences may be very grave. During my ministry I have noticed manifestations of the worst effects in cases when one of the parents cursed his children or a grandparent cursed his grandchildren. If the curse is uttered against a person's happiness or success in life, the results have awful consequences.

Curses uttered on special occasions such as weddings, for example, carry a specific weight, and vary in consequences: continuous illnesses that follow one throughout life, numerous difficulties at work throughout one's whole life, misfortunes in marriage, illness of children...The reason for this lies in the existing blood bond between a parent and a child which overlaps with the question of authority. Some mothers curse their children out of bad habit. They damn them to hell without attaching real meaning to it. Whatever the case may be, the devil obeys and as soon as someone leaves the door ajar, he rushes in and won't readily get out. Jesus himself said: *"I assure you, on judgment day people will be held accountable for every unguarded word they speak. By your words you will be acquitted, and by your words you will be condemned."* (Mt 12:36–37)

Satanism

The depravity of man in modern times seems limitless. We witness an increased number of people professionally involved in black magic, spiritism and satanic cults, eager to communicate their 'message' to the people. The unscrupulous lucrative profit motive plays a dominant role and motivation in all this.

Many people consider magician Aleister Crowley (1875–1947) to be the greatest Satanist of the twentieth century. He thought himself to be the Antichrist and called himself 'The Big Beast 666,' 'The Beast of the Abyss.' (cf. Rev. 11:7) He was convinced that the occult, magic forces of supernatural knowledge and abilities wanted to use him as a channel for communication with mankind. He described the purpose of his mission: "… to set in motion the occult forces which will culminate in the enlightenment of all people at the end of this century." Due to his influence, the whole dark world of mysterious rituals and secret occult lodges developed in which black magic, worshipping of the devil and weird sacrifices are practised, including sometimes even human sacrifices. Aleister Crowley made a strong impact on many people whom he placed under the influence of the Evil One. Today Crowley's books are sold in the tens of thousands.

Holy Scripture tells us clearly of the apostasy of many from God before the second coming of Jesus. *"Let no one seduce you, no matter how. Since the mass apostasy has not yet occurred nor the man of lawlessness been revealed—that son of perdition and adversary who exalts himself above every so-called god proposed for worship, he who seats himself in God's temple and even declares himself to be God—do you not remember how I used to tell you about these things when I was still with you?"* (2 Thes. 2:3–5) *"The coming of the Son of Man will repeat what happened in Noah's time. In the days before the flood people were eating and drinking, marrying and being married, right up to the day Noah entered the ark. They were totally unconcerned until the flood came and destroyed them. So will it be at the coming of the Son of Man."* (Mt. 24:37–39) This apostasy of which the Bible speaks is connected with the ascendancy of lawlessness i.e. the renunciation of God's order: *"and because of the increase of evil, the love of most will grow cold."* (Mt. 24:12) If we take a look at our world today, we will have to affirm that this has been happening for some time now, even among those who call themselves Christians. Only the testimony of true believers and the effective power of the Holy Spirit are postponing the coming of the final disaster. (cf. Rev. 9:20–21) Is it not evident that the hearts of many are hardened towards God and His Word? Some people are hindered from turning to God because of their 'enlightened' scientific and philosophic accomplishments. Their pride is blocking them from seeing the Truth.

As a result, they go to the opposite extreme, putting their trust and worship in their favorite idols: gold idols — economic power; brass idols — technology and armaments; stone idols — massive buildings.

Promiscuity, thefts and murders are found everywhere and have become part of our daily existence. Premarital and extramarital relationships are considered common occurrences. The wave of pornography is so engulfing that there are no longer any magazines or attractive advertisements without pornographic images. The American media inform us that a murder is committed in the USA every 23 minutes, an armed robbery takes place every 75 seconds and a burglary occurs every 10 seconds.

The worshipping of demons and magic has reached horrible dimensions today.

We will not deal here with the worshipping of the spirit of Time (Zeit Geist), ideologies and idols. I am referring here primarily to a spiritual disaster of apocalyptical proportions that has come crashing down on mankind in full strength. Every day there is more interest in occultism and parapsychology. In the USA, more than a hundred colleges offer courses in parapsychology, not to mention the large amount of literature in the fields of astrology, magic and witchcraft. Every year millions of young people join magical sects of all types.

In recent times the workings of the Devil have increased exceptionally. It is not just one person affected, but through that one person, the whole of society, nations and countries are affected as well. Satan constantly manifests his presence in deadly wars, maltreatment, killings of the unborn, various forms of Satanism, disappearance of consciences and morals with which we can differentiate good from evil, or in more powerful riots against God, religion, morality, truth, dignity, law, order and understanding. All of this can be seen not only in social, economical and political life but also in the world of culture, literature, art and entertainment.

Modern theology that is increasingly oriented towards rationalism, materialism and the matters of this world contributes on its own to the flourishing of the occult, which is a paradox in itself. Author and social critic Os Guinness astutely observed this fact when he wrote: "Christianity which has begun to look upon the occult as a non-existent dimension lost its central position in between those who denied the reality of these phenomena and those who openly and wholly acknowledged it. Therefore, anyone who looked for the spiritual dimension — and could not find it in the Church — turned to occultism. It is an ironic fact that the theologians who have lulled themselves into the rationalism of their thought are the last to believe in the occult phenomena."

Peter Bayerhaus, a renowned theologian, perceiving this demonic invasion which has been increasing every day in our age, explicitly demands that:

The wave of the occult in its different forms and satanic background should not be regarded as innocuous.

We should confront the surge of occultism with the utmost vigilance in our spiritual life.

Considering the surge of occultism, true Christians should apprehend their calling more consciously so that in the spiritual combat they would choose the side of light.

Satanism in Rock Music

Someone probably will be surprised and ask: Is it possible for the Evil One to exert influence on people through music? Is it not unreasonable to say that?

From the previous paragraphs it is evident how Satanism has become a disquieting phenomenon, spreading rapidly all over the whole world, particularly in last years of the 20th century and the beginning of the 21st century. Young people living idle, empty lives, without sensible ideals and craving novelties and adventures, find that the occult is the most interesting ambience to suit their unaccomplished ambitions. Satan has excellent insight into the psychology of young people who question all the established values. Thus he entices in them an urge to overturn and distort everything that has been preserved and sacred up to now. In like manner, Satan wants to deride and desecrate the Eucharist, which is the focal point of our faith. The so-called 'black masses' are well known in Satanism and, regretfully, have many devotees in our homeland as well. They also have an 'altar' on which they perform an abominable rite: during the 'mass' they recite specific, twisted prayers and the participants turn to Satan and praise him as their god. The culmination of the 'black mass' certainly occurs during 'communion' in which the stolen consecrated hosts are mixed with the blood of the sacrificed animal that the participants are to drink. This satanic act coincides with sexual orgies that are expected to procure magical strength. If a woman conceives a baby during such an intercourse, she is obligated to give birth in secrecy and sacrifice the child to Satan. The Satanists maintain that this type of sacrifice is the one that pleases Satan the most. So during these secretive séances, they offer animals, humans and even children as altar sacrifices to appease the Evil One. It is a notorious fact that some artists, especially musicians, have a tendency to get involved in black magic, spiritism and satanic cults. The most prominent application of these practices can currently be found in hard rock and heavy metal music, especially on stage. Curiously enough, the lives of the rock stars are hidden and veiled with mystery.

The powerful diffusion of the occult and satanic cults through rock music began precisely after 1969 when the era of "worshipping the devil" was proclaimed, along with the establishment of the first satanic church in San Francisco. The beginning of the overt worshipping of Satan is connected with the English band 'Black Sabbath', which became the forerunner of the young generation of heavy metal bands. These promoted the occult, magic, spiritism, and Satanism, especially through lyrics. Their shocking lyrics reaped great success with the young under-age audience, such as: "Take a life, it's going cheap; Kill someone, no one will weep; Freedom's yours, just pay your dues, we just want your soul to use" (The 'Cornucopia' song from the album 'Vol. 4', 1972).

Anton Szandor LaVey, an enthusiastic worshipper of Satan and founder of the first Satanic church in the USA, declared in 1968: "The multitude which follows evil perverts the Lord's prayer, mixes it with obscene words, kicks Christ's cross with their feet or hangs it upside down." We read the following words on the cover of the LP record "Reflection – Black Sabbath": "On the first LP they immediately conjured up Satan who appeared indeed. He promised they would have success all over the world if only they would play on the great Sabbath every year. Both parties have kept their word up to the present time." The covers of their LP records show the notorious number 666, the number of the Antichrist (cf. Rev. 13:18); the imprints of the skull and crossbones on T-shirts are worn by the fan clubs as an open sign of their adherence to Satanism. In some songs they call Satan "Lord of this world."

A known Christian expert of rock music in the USA writes: "I was shocked to discover that disturbingly large numbers of young people who believe in Christ buy and listen to Black Sabbath albums, even though they know this band favors Satan."

Another very famous, world-renowned rock band is the Rolling Stones. How the Evil One operates through them is evident by what happened on December 6, 1969 at an abandoned automobile speedway near San Francisco. The Stones were holding a free rock festival there. More than 300,000 people were present. When they started to sing 'Carol,' several young people took all their clothes off and crawled onto the stage, the 'main altar,' wanting to offer themselves as a sacrifice. The bouncers responsible for order at the concert were the Hell's Angels, who started to beat these young people atrociously, as if driven by some supernatural force. Not only did these young people accept the pain and the brutality but they demanded to be beaten more ferociously. When the Stones played "Sympathy for the Devil," the bouncers started to kick the audience at random. At this point the bloody fight was out of control and could not be stopped. Three people were killed, about twenty serious incidents were reported and many people were injured. One of the fans who was driving a car at a great speed smashed into the crowd, killing two young people. A young man high on LSD drowned in the canal, another one's leg caught fire and was taken to hospital with serious burns. About twenty physicians and six psychiatrists spent exhausting hours treating drug addicts, premature childbirth and fighting injuries. These are explicit examples of how Satan can exert a horrible influence on the masses of people through rock music. When Satanism is promoted through rock music, negative incidents always follow: suicides, violence of every type, intake of drugs and alcohol, disordered sexuality, hatred, insolence, pornography, robbery, egoism, racism, anarchy, fanaticism and perversities of every kind. Whenever music and singing urge one to overstep the limits of normal human behavior causing vandalism, then we can be certain that this sort of music and lyrics lead one to hell.

The members of rock bands often give statements that blatantly indicate the surroundings in which they live. Glen Bertan, singer and bass guitarist of the death-metal band Deicide, says: "I believe in just a few things: hate everyone, kill your enemies, death for all those who oppose you, think only of yourself and believe only in yourself. When I was a boy I was forced to go to church and I always resisted; everything connected to the church and Christianity disgusted me. Rotten Christians, for example, are bothered by the fact that I have a distinct satanic image and the satanic cross imprinted on my forehead. I did it just because I liked it. Nobody told me I had to do it but if you want to prove something in life, you just act on it by making a sign that you will carry around all your life. Do I believe in God or in Satan? The fact is that God cast Satan out of heaven and hurled him down on earth to become master of the world. As for me I think that Satan is God just as Jehovah is God."

Anton LaVey, father of the first satanic church and its first high priest, developed his own philosophy of modern Satanism with the Nine Satanic declarations as the antithesis to the biblical commandments.

When young people adopt satanic norms of behavior we should not wonder at the alarming news that is reaching us every day and happening more and more: orgies in the graveyards, rape, desecration of tombs, and human and animal sacrifices. There is also news about fires in churches and ritual murders among young people.

Music has an enormous influence on man. That has been known for some time. Some types of music can bring about a state of trance or create an atmosphere favoring the working of evil spirits. Music can change man's moods and that is precisely what the magic and occult practices are aiming for. Persons in a trance are often aggressively disposed or do some sexual activity that they would not do if they were in a normal state of mind. To be more precise, in a state of trance a person is psychically impotent, which is why it is possible to exert a powerful influence over him.

At rock concerts and in disco clubs the whining sounds of electronically amplified guitars and the frenzied beating of drums that agitate the nerves enable rock and beat-musicians to transform young people into howling monsters. One physician said: "In this state of mind the loss of bodily functions takes place. The state of trance, accompanied by spasmodic and epileptic quivers, screaming, biting, laughter, urinating and tearing off of clothes, is experienced as happiness and pleasure."

Bob Larson was an active rock musician before he came to believe in Jesus Christ and was deeply concerned because of the horrible facts he had discovered during his investigations: "Satan knows that if he wants to be effective in the end times before the second coming of Jesus, he has to gain control over young people. Satan uses hard rock to overcome young generations in a massive degree. I have seen with my own eyes how demons would possess young people while dancing to the beat of rock music. This was specifically visible with young girls. A person would expect a young lady to retain a certain decency while dancing but, on the contrary, I have witnessed how young girls would plunge into spasmodic convulsions, which could only be explained as a manifestation of diabolical activity. Some kind of fear would seize me watching these occurrences taking place while they were dancing to the tunes of my music."

Taking all these facts into account, we should conclude that very loud music with deafening rhythm, constantly 'charged atmosphere' of scents, darkness, intermittent switching of colors and a lightning of flash lights, the multitude of listeners that suggestively have an effect on each other — all these signs are found at rock concerts and disco clubs where Satan reaps an abundant harvest of victims who are in a state of intoxication and confusion.

Immodesty in Dress

Many people will ask: "Is it really possible that evil spirits can influence people even through the mode of dress?"

It is confirmed through everyday practice that the dress code of a person can certainly be provocative and in a particular way an occasion where Satan in a 'modern, contemporary and refined' fashion can induce people to sin.

The style of dress discloses not only the taste but also the moral standards of a person. To dress attractively, delightfully and fashionably is not a bad thing in itself. On the contrary, it undoubtedly shows refinement of character and a keen sense of beauty. A pleasing classical style is always suitable for various occasions and situations in contemporary living, for it is proper as long as it follows certain guidelines.

The female world is especially subject to an exhibitionist way of dressing, for it is under the heavy influence of the present trend that is promoted by the mass media. The mass media want to create a general opinion of how absolute freedom is predominant in fashion, regardless of Christian moral principles. "Who cares about them in today's world?" is their motto. According to the contemporary culture that is persistently being imposed on us, there is nothing whatsoever unnatural or ugly, least of all, sinful. Immodesty in dress is aimed at awakening the surges of corporal lust and sexual instinct in the opposite sex.

Psychological analyses of this particular behavior show that often we are dealing with very insecure and unstable persons who do not have self-confidence. Therefore, by dressing indecently, they will get another person's attention. Shameless exposure of the breasts, the navel and other parts of the body is meant to prove that there is nothing whatsoever that belongs exclusively to one's intimacy.

Nowadays 'modern' girls are seen more often walking in lingerie than in clothes, with deep-cut décolletage, long skirt slits running up to the waist, mini-skirts and shorts. Despite the warning signs on many church doors that clearly prohibit the entrance of indecently-dressed individuals, it is not uncommon for a girl dressed in this manner to enter a church and attend Mass, even to receive Holy Communion. The Basilica of St. Peter in Rome and many other churches have guards who warn and prevent indecently dressed persons from entering holy places. This does not mean that a girl ought to enter the church in an old, outdated dress, sagging on her as if it was hung on a hanger. There are indeed many ways in which a girl can dress trendily and modestly in clothes that fit her nicely and becomingly.

Reading this, many girls will probably say how they usually don't think anything bad and simply want to look young and beautiful in a modern way. True enough. However, are these girls aware of what others think and what thoughts and desires they entice in those looking at them dressed in a provocative manner? One should have a refined dignity and humility in dress and not make of oneself a display window for curious passers-by to peruse at will and at any time. Every Christian girl should discover her own personal style of dress that will help her feel at ease on every occasion and at any place. Otherwise, she should be aware that whoever looks at her with lust or evil intentions whether in a plane, on the street or in a bus, takes away a tiny portion of her inner peace and innocent soul. It could be true that such a girl may not entertain any evil intentions in her mind but she should in no way draw others to harbor evil thoughts.

Perhaps it would be a good idea if our girls would ask themselves how the Blessed Virgin Mary would dress if she were a girl of our time. Surely it would be something contemporary, not eye-catching, and in a style that would show the beauty of a woman as a person and not just the beauty of the female's body parts. Modesty and decency are the virtues that somehow everyone is able to determine for oneself.

Regretfully, we stopped talking about this topic at catechism classes and during sermons. We should continually teach young people how to adopt the right attitude and moral standpoint; we should pinpoint all the possible outcomes in case we neglect this topic. Our younger generation should be witnessing for Jesus Christ with their lives. I dare pose this question: "Who will believe a witness who is walking down the streets half-naked, even entering a church in this manner?"

All of us should teach and educate, with love, the younger generation about this issue, starting from parents to catechists and priests. For the Evil One is deftly pulling into his venomous webs large numbers of souls every day and is harvesting abundant fruit. He enjoys it most when he succeeds with young people who are the carriers of life.

How to Free Oneself from Satan's Influence

After extensive description of most of the snares which Satan employs in his cunning seduction of men, it is natural to ask ourselves: Is there a way out? In particular those who, consciously or not, have stepped into the territory of the evil spirits and have been exposed to the negative and demonic forces ask this question. However, today many people fit into this category. There are those who, in their innermost being, feel as if they are imprisoned in a vicious circle, imprisoning them inside. No matter what they do, it does not help them. They feel they are being dominated by a higher force they cannot resist or expel. They roam from place to place looking for help and deliverance from this grip.

I believe that many come not only to my door every day but to the doors of many priests as well, pressed by their troubles and anxieties, looking for salvation. This book has been written with a heartfelt intention to help especially those who find themselves in dire circumstances, who have already given into despair, given up every hope, as well as for many others out there seeking assistance.

I would like to emphasize again the fact that Satan is stronger than man. When man approaches him and enters his territory he feels helpless. Man cannot oppose evil on his own.

There is no possibility of his counteracting this evil with his own strength. Yet another fundamental truth is far more significant: God is infinitely stronger than Satan! The only possibility of tearing apart the evil web is rooted in this truth. Only Divine power is able to overcome evil; only Divine light, the light of the Holy Spirit, is able to reveal the wiles and intrigues of Satan. If we are tightly pressed to our God, Satan cannot harm us in any way. We just have to believe strongly that we can always defeat Satan with God's grace, for God is our help and stronghold.

This is clearly written in the Catechism of the Catholic Church: "The power of Satan is, nonetheless, not infinite. He is only a creature, powerful from the fact that he is a pure spirit, but still a creature. He cannot prevent the building up of God's reign. Although Satan may act in the world out of hatred for God and his kingdom in Christ Jesus, and although his action may cause grave injuries — of a spiritual nature and, indirectly, even of a physical nature — to man and to society, the action is permitted by divine providence which, with strength and gentleness, guides human and cosmic history. It is a great mystery that providence should permit diabolical activity, but 'we know that in everything God works for good with those who love him.'" (CCC 395; Rom. 8:28)

David defeated the giant Goliath in the name of the Lord Almighty using his slingshot and a stone. We shall likewise overthrow the powers of evil in the name of Jesus and in the name of His most Holy Mother Mary.

Jesus Christ — the Only Deliverer and Healer

Reading attentively through the Gospels we come to the conclusion that most of the accounts are centered on Jesus' ministry of healing. Immediately after His baptism in the river Jordan, Jesus was filled with the power of the Holy Spirit and began His public ministry. He testified openly that He is the fulfillment of Isaiah's prophecies. He was sent by God to heal the sick and deliver those oppressed by the devil. (cf. Lk. 4:18)

Wanting to be assured that Jesus was the promised Messiah, John the Baptist sent his disciples to ask Jesus if He was the One or should they expect another one to come. Jesus said to the disciples: "*Go back and report to John what you hear and see: the blind recover their sight, cripples walk, lepers are cured, the deaf hear, dead men are raised to life, and the poor have the good news preached to them.*" (Mt. 11:5) Luke's Gospel reads: "*Coming down the mountain with them, he stopped at a level stretch where there were many of his disciples; a large crowd of people was with them from all Judea and Jerusalem and the coast of Tyre and Sidon, people who came to hear him and be healed of their diseases. Those who were troubled with unclean spirits were cured; indeed, the whole crowd was trying to touch him because power went out from him which cured all.*" (Lk. 6:17-19) Mark's Gospel reads: "*Those whom he cured, who were variously afflicted, were many, and so were the demons expelled.*" (Mk. 1:34) Jesus called His disciples to continue to do what He had been doing: He entrusted them with the ministry of delivering and healing: "*Then he summoned his twelve disciples and gave them authority to expel unclean spirits and to cure sickness and disease of every kind."* (Mt. 10:1) The same authority and power of healing and rebuking the evil spirits was appointed to the seventy-two disciples by Jesus in Luke 10, verses 1-8.

In Matthew's Gospel we find the famous account where a father brought his son, who was epileptic and possessed by an unclean spirit, before Jesus' disciples so that they could heal him. Since the disciples could not heal the boy, Jesus cured the boy instantly by commanding the evil spirit to leave the boy. Then the disciples asked Jesus why they could not drive the evil spirit out. Jesus replied: *"'Because you have so little trust,' he told them. 'I assure you, if you had faith the size of a mustard seed, you would be able to say to this mountain, 'Move from here to there,' and it would move. Nothing would be impossible for you [This kind does not leave but by prayer and fasting.]'"* (Mt. 17:20-21) *"This kind you can drive out only by prayer."* (Mk. 9:29)

The Gospels testify to the fact that the apostles and disciples began their ministry at the same time that Jesus was fulfilling His public mission on earth. *"The seventy-two returned in jubilation saying, 'Master, even the demons are subject to us in your name.'"* (Lk. 10:17)

After the Resurrection, Jesus gave to many of the faithful the power to heal the sick and drive out demons: *"And these signs will accompany those who have professed their faith: They will use my name to expel demons…and the sick upon whom they lay their hands will recover."* (Mk. 16: 17-18)

Bearing in mind all the biblical references, we can conclude that, beyond a shred of doubt, Jesus carried out the ministry of healing which He passed onto His disciples. This very fact makes it hard to understand why Jesus' disciples today, bishops and priests, with a certain reticence and inexplicable distrust, give no importance to this extremely significant and necessary ministry in the Church. Therefore, it is quite understandable that many of those who have not received a warm welcome and understanding from their spiritual shepherds go and visit inviting but dangerous witch doctors, who deal with esoteric and various magical practices, i.e. satanic practices, and thus plunge only deeper into Satan's pit of imprisonment and ruin.

In my many years of experience in the ministry of deliverance, I can testify to a number of deliverances and healings that have taken place at seminars and retreats that I have conducted. Above all, I can testify with confidence that even a greater number of healings and deliverances, both spiritual and physical, have occurred during Holy

Mass and adoration of the Blessed Sacrament than on occasions when we priests would lay our hands on people. Miracles at Lourdes are happening during the Eucharistic procession, which is quite natural since the Eucharist is the sacrament of restoration. Whoever receives it unworthily will bring upon himself judgment and condemnation, (cf. 1 Cor. 11:29) whereas whoever receives the Body worthily brings upon himself the restoration of the body and the soul. Before receiving Holy Communion, we pray: "Lord, I am not worthy that you should enter under my roof, but only say the word and my soul shall be healed."

It is crucial to mention that it is Jesus who heals, even if He does so through His anointed servants bestowed with the gifts of faith and healing. In the whole history of the Church, as well as today, there has always been a number of anointed faithful whom God has gifted with the charism of healing. It must be repeated that it is Jesus Himself who operates through His servants, helping, healing and delivering the faithful.

An excellent illustration of this is found in the story of the crippled man who was healed at the gate of the Temple. The witnesses to this event thought that Peter and John healed the man, after which Peter addressed them: *"Fellow Israelites, why does this surprise you? Why do you stare at us as if we had made this man walk by some power or holiness of our own? The God of Abraham, of Isaac, and of Jacob, the God of our fathers, has glorified his Servant Jesus, whom you handed down and disowned in Pilate's presence when Pilate was ready to release him. You disowned the Holy and Just One and preferred instead to be granted the release of a murderer. You put to death the Author of life. But God raised him from the dead, and we are his witnesses. It is his name, and trust in this name, that has strengthened the limbs of this man whom you see and know well. Such faith has given him perfect health, as all of you can observe."* (Acts 3:12-16) Therefore, it is essential to notice and keep in mind the fact that when people are healed, IT IS ALWAYS JESUS WHO HEALS THEM through the laying on of hands and prayers of His anointed servants.

Practical Guidelines and Advice

What must one do when one has entered into the area of evil and does not see the way out?

My advice is: make it imperative to visit an experienced priest who will, with God's power, help you to break away from these chains. *"Jesus summoned the Twelve and began to send them out two by two giving them authority over unclean spirits."* (Mk. 6:7) *"With that they went off, preaching repentance. They expelled many demons, anointed the sick and worked many cures."* (Mk. 6:12-13) Priests have the very same authority today, provided that one believes in one's priesthood and the powers which the Lord bestows. I am not talking about conducting the ministry of exorcism, which is the last resort with extreme cases because the rite of exorcism can be conducted only and solely by a priest who has explicit authorization from his bishop. My point is that these cases are few indeed. Renowned and experienced exorcists reckon that from all the cases where they recognized evident manifestation of the evil spirit, only two percent are real classical cases of diabolical possession, in which case the rite of exorcism is the only effective outcome. All other cases could be successfully resolved by an experienced priest. The good Pope John XXIII particularly singled out St. John Vianney, the parish priest, who wrestled out many souls from Satan's shackles even though he was not an exorcist and had never conducted the rite of exorcism in his life. Every priest has many means at his disposal which he should employ in his ministry of delivering souls from the snares of the devil.

Faith is needed, trust in Jesus is needed, for He defeated Satan and crushed his kingdom. And today Jesus Christ is the same. The enemy forces flee at the sight of His Cross. If our faith is strong, every evil influence or satanic presence must disappear through the power of His Name.

We have the Immaculate Virgin at our side. She is a conqueror over Satan, always willing to preserve, protect and sustain us in our earthly battle against satanic influences of all kinds. She is at our aid and assistance, together with the intercession of St. Michael and all the angels and saints in heaven.

Satanic influence and its malignant impact on people are manifested in situations when one distances oneself from God, which many people have experienced in their lives. It frequently happens that one starts to forsake and neglect daily prayer, Sunday observances, regular confession. Slowly and imperceptibly, he yields before temptations and seductions and, without being aware of what is happening, he suddenly falls under Satan's influence, who masterly entangles him into his web, darkening his mind, weakening his will, reducing him to a state of utter powerlessness to put up any fight against evil. For that person, we should first pray that God may, through the gift of faith, strengthen his faith, open up his spiritual eyes and shed light onto his condition. I would also recommend to that person in need to pray himself as well, sincerely and deeply from his heart, which he can express with these or similar words: **"Jesus, My Lord, have mercy on me. I am sorry for all the sins I have committed. I despise all my sins and sinful occasions. I kindly ask you to forgive me. Wash me in your Precious Blood. My Lord and My God, have pity on me, a sinner. My soul thirsts and longs for your Holy Spirit. Fill me with your Spirit so powerfully that I may be cleansed, healed and saved. Thank you, Jesus; I praise you, Jesus!"** If he feels hatred or animosity towards anyone, he should strive to forgive those while praying.

What should be done in this and similar cases?

Exorcists recommend the following instruments: the Sacrament of Reconciliation; Holy Communion; in special cases, the Sacrament of the Anointing of the Sick; acts of penance and conversion; as well as various prayers for physical healing and psychological deliverance. They strongly recommend giving priority to the Sacrament of Reconciliation. Satan fears it the most because in it there is an immediate effectiveness of the 'Precious Blood of Jesus' which washes away and cleanses every sin, becoming an armor of protection against the infernal foe.

In most cases, the confession of one's whole life is critical. It is essential to make a thorough revision of one's life with God's help and in His light. This can be done only with a sincere prayer, with the light of the Holy Spirit who reveals and unmasks all the hidden and disguised snares of the Evil One. At the end of this book there is a detailed outline of the examination of conscience so that a good and valid confession can be made; this is useful to the person who has a desire to obtain an insight into the real condition of his conscience and to unmask the tricks of the devil that will unburden his soul, reconcile it to God and restore his inner peace. Let this be the occasion where the person stands at a crossroad in life, a point of making a decision as to which course to choose.

If one wants to break free from the bondage of the Evil One, it is essential to renounce the devil resolutely and irrevocably. One should renounce the devil himself, all of his seductions and adulatory offers and any 'assistance' that could come through his influence. His entire trust has to be surrendered to God; man should abandon himself entirely into God's hands and consciously entrust his life to Him so that He may guide and rule it. Accept Jesus as your Lord. *"There is no salvation in anyone else, for there is no other name in the whole world given to men by which we are to be saved"* (Acts 4:12) The evil spirit will swiftly take advantage of any wavering or indecisiveness and hurl him into an even more critical situation. *"No man can serve two masters;"* (Mt. 6:24) *"Whoever puts his hand to the plow but keeps looking back is unfit for the reign of God."* (Lk. 9:62)

And then in the Sacrament of the Eucharist we receive the Body and the Blood of Christ, who gives us His life and strength to confront every attack from evil spirits. We, in effect, live on Jesus, who is our sole Redeemer and Savior, who has come into this world for the specific reason to destroy the work of the devil.

The Holy Mass makes present Christ's sacrifice by which Satan has been vanquished. By receiving Christ in the Eucharist we receive the One who has crushed Satan's power, the One whose power is immense and whose protection is the most effective against the onslaughts of the Evil One. Satan is completely powerless before Him. That is why it is highly recommended to those who have been delivered from the bondage of the Evil One to attend and participate actively in the Eucharistic celebration and to receive Christ in Communion several times a week or as often as possible. After the absolute renunciation of evil and definite termination of all satanic practices, after a well-observed Sacrament of Reconciliation, God washes away every sin from man, through His Son Jesus Christ, and re-establishes friendship with him.

Then the priest will pray the prayer of deliverance from the Ritual over an inflicted person so that God may deliver him through the prayer of the Church from any evil influence that may have saturated a person through personal participation in any magical practice during his life.

Sacramentals include public and private prayers which can be efficiently used for different psychological or physical problems. The Church has a special booklet called "Blessings." This prayer book is assembled from various blessing prayers which are not sacraments. However, if they are prayed with faith and if a person for whom the prayers are intended is truly converted, believing that the Lord will grant him deliverance through these prayers, only then will the prayers recommended by the Church have their visible effect.

There are also prayers of deliverance, for the evil spirit has to be expelled. I would like to put emphasis on one vital precondition that this prayer should be always done fully conscious in the name of Jesus. Therefore, the prime prerequisite is to have faith in Jesus' power because *"there is no salvation in anyone else, for there is no other name in the whole world given to men by which we are to be saved."* (Acts 4:12) Consequently the authority of deliverance comes down directly from Jesus Christ who carefully observes mostly the faith of a deprecator as well as the faith of the person for whom the prayers are intended. Faith of the relatives and friends who are praying for the specific person is taken into account as well. I would like to recall the amazing healing story that we find in the Gospel of the paralyzed man, which put emphasis on the faith of the bearers who brought before Jesus the paralytic through the housetop and Jesus, having seen their faith, (Lk. 5:20) wrought a miracle.

Once the yoke of the evil spirit is thrown off, it is extremely important that the person continue to live a life in grace, which means to strive to live in faithfulness to Christ and in constant struggle against the schemes of the Evil One who will use every strategy to recapture his prey. A person has to be aware of the fact that every time, with God's help, he must say 'YES' to Christ and 'NO' to Satan. Since this is just the beginning of the walk, one should not falter here because what the Gospel has warned us about may happen: *"When the unclean spirit departs from a man, it roams through arid wastes searching for a place of rest and finding none. Then it says, 'I will go back where I came from,' and returns to find the dwelling unoccupied, though swept and tidied now. Off it goes again to bring back with it this time seven spirits more evil than itself. Thus the last state of that man becomes worse than the first."* (Mt. 12:43-45) Therefore, the soul must not be left empty, even though it is purified after having gone through a good confession. This is not enough. What is necessary is to persevere in praying every day, keeping in mind that we alone are helpless against evil. The Lord is our only strength and mighty protection against evil.

For this particular reason, it is important to dedicate some time for personal prayer and to enter into communion with the Lord in earnest prayer, which would be best to observe at the same time every day. One should put forth an effort and allow the prayer to become part of one's being. Just as one is thirsty and hungry for food at certain times of the day, likewise one should hunger for daily prayer. It is particularly important to implore in our prayers that the Blood of Christ defend us from every negative impact of Satan's wickedness. We will always feel the great power and protection if we have recourse to the Immaculate Heart of our heavenly Mother. Mother Mary is the eternal enemy of the devil: *"I will put enmity between you and the woman."* (Gen. 3:15) She is the one who will ultimately crush his head. Her heart will triumph, celebrating the victory over Satan. Whenever an evil spirit renews his enticements and one begins to yield to temptations, one can obtain particular help by praying to St. Michael the Archangel, the chief of the heavenly hosts who hurled Lucifer and his minions into the abyss of hell.

If you have wholeheartedly decided to follow Jesus, you should find some time to dedicate yourself to the reading of the Scriptures. God's Word is truly the light for our life and path. (Ps. 119:105) Saint Augustine used to say that ignorance of Scripture in itself is ignorance of God for it is so clear that we can love Jesus only if we know Him for who He is.

The collective family prayer is vitally important and effective. There is an old saying: 'the family that prays together stays together.' Lack of communal prayer in the family is very often the cause for a number of divorces and conflicts among family members. A husband and wife of contrasting character traits can stay together only with God's help.

If family prayer is nourished, the children will grow in the healthy ambience of a genuine Christian spirituality. The rosary is a highly recommended prayer for every family as the nucleus of family prayer.

Another important recommendation is that a person should join a prayer group in order to grow in his spiritual life. The prayer group usually gathers for weekly prayer, which brings an enormous boost to members of the group, uplifting them in the love of God and in the service of others.

Remove from your house every negative piece of literature, videos of bad and often scandalous content, bad music; in fact, burn all of the bad things in your house that might draw your children away from God's path. Do not give way to tempting opportunity. Be cautious as to how you use the Internet or television. You can use them but not abuse them. Choose for yourself a spiritual director, a priest with some experience in spiritual issues, who will assist and direct you in real and concrete situations in your life. You should open your soul, without any hindrance, fear or prejudices, to your spiritual director with confidence that his advice can be helpful for your progress in leading a virtuous life. It would be meritorious if you would confess to him regularly and thus enable him to supervise your spiritual growth by advising you properly.

Try to engage yourself actively in the life of your parish community. Effective participation in parish activities will assist you in growing in your Christian maturity and holiness. Perhaps becoming involved in evangelization or joining the church choir, visiting elderly parishioners, the sick, prisoners, etc. will help you in some way.

Man's spirit that has been weakened by negative practices has to be gradually strengthened through sacrifice, self-denial and fasting. These are fruitful means for our spiritual growth. Unfortunately, these fruitful practices have become incomprehensible and weird to contemporary man. The hedonistic mentality deeply implanted in our being has made us weaklings who are keen only on fulfilling our every desire, and every self-denial has become gibberish which contemporary man, especially the younger generation, is not able to comprehend. This is why the evil spirit exerts an immense influence over people in these times. Jesus clearly explained what one should do in case of serious satanic forces being inflicted on man: *"This kind you can drive out only by prayer [and fasting]."* (Mk. 9:29) People who have truly embraced Jesus' recommendation and start implementing it in their lives, surely have felt the effectiveness and the truth of His advice.

Vows are inherent to Christian spirituality. Namely, when we ask the Lord to grant us a grace, He puts us through the test because He wants to see how deep our faith is, and the faith is proven through deeds. St. James said in his epistle: *"My brothers, what good is it to profess faith without practising it? ... So it is with the faith that does nothing in practice. It is thoroughly lifeless... Faith without works is as dead as a body without breath."* (James 2:14,17,26) God is continually testing us and watching closely for our willingness to respond. He highly respects and rewards abundantly every act of our love, even the smallest one, every generous submission from our part. We cannot supersede Him in His generosity. Every gift, even the smallest one, offered out of love for Him or for our neighbor, He repays a hundredfold: *"Give, and and it shall be given to you. Good measure pressed down, shaken together, running over, will they pour into the fold of your garment. For the measure you measure with will be measured back to you."* (Lk. 6:38)

I would like to mention also a special form of Christian piety — pilgrimages. In Israel, the ancient people of God often went on pilgrimages. Pilgrimages hold a prominent place with the New People of God, in the Church of Christ. Pope John Paul II in his papal bull "The Mystery of the Incarnation," announced the Jubilee Year 2000 and specifically singled out pilgrimages to remind each one of us that our life on earth is a journey. Pilgrimages exercise the faithful in practical asceticism, stirring in them sincere repentance for their weaknesses, allowing them to gain a deeper insight into their waywardness and temptations. Thus many individuals who set out in earnest on a pilgrimage undergo an interior change and renewal of heart. Through vigils, prayer and fasting, a pilgrim progresses along the path of Christian perfection. (Cf. "The Mystery of the Incarnation" no.7)

The Catholic Church offers us another outstanding means of assistance on our path to Christian perfection through the gift of forgiveness. Our heavenly Father, in His abundant mercy, welcomes us with His love manifested in the forgiveness of sins through the Sacrament of Reconciliation. God leans down to every human weakness in order to enfold man in the embrace of His mercy. Through Christ's sacrifice and through the Sacrament of Penance we are given the grace to reconcile with God and we obtain His forgiveness, which results in a true change and renewal of our life. We are being granted the forgiveness from 'eternal punishment.' However, on particular days and occasions determined by the Church, God in His love grants us the remission of 'temporal punishment' for our sins which we have deserved either on this earth or in Purgatory so that one day we will be able to enter into the fullness of communion with God and our brothers and sisters.

God is the source of all blessing. All good comes from Him. From ancient times God allowed his people, in particular, patriarchs, kings, priests, Levites and parents to bless other people in His name.

The Church of Christ also follows the steps of this tradition, praising and blessing God for His gifts and for rebuking the reign of the Evil One in the world. The Church blesses persons, objects and places. The blessings of the Church are liturgical acts by which, through the prescribed prayers of the Church and its faith, a blessing is bestowed through a man but not from a man. The Church has published an official liturgical booklet called "Blessings" with an abundant treasure of blessing prayers that can be used by ministers of the Church and the faithful laity. Blessings are not sacraments, but sacramentals, and the stronger the faith is, the more efficacious they are. The use of blessings is not efficacious if one does not have faith. The Second Vatican Council and the Code of Canon Law (CCL 1166) define sacramentals as "sacred signs which in a sense imitate the sacraments. They signify certain effects, especially spiritual ones, and they achieve these effects through the intercession of the Church." Whoever uses sacramentals with faith often obtains surprising results. In many cases one can drive away completely satanic illusions or disclose satanic deeds with blessings.

It is a praiseworthy custom among the faithful to take holy water into their homes with reverence so that by using it in faith they may protect themselves, their children, the places in which they live and work. Many faithful want to have certain pious objects blessed including crosses, pictures, rosaries, medals, believing that through the blessing imparted on these objects the Lord protects them from all evil and negative influence.

It is necessary to impart a particular blessing on dwelling places, apartments, houses...where satanic deeds, especially spiritistic séances, satanic cults or any other form of occult or magic practices have been performed. Magical objects like amulets, statues of certain pagan gods/deities, magical and occult books that are given by sorcerers or similar things for 'protection,' should be sprinkled with holy water and burnt so that all satanic influence may be annihilated. Other symbols of superstition which many people think bring good luck (the signs of the zodiac, horseshoes, four-leaf clovers, little elephants, whales...) should be discarded by the same procedure previously mentioned. While performing these recommended steps of procedure, one should pray and act in full faith, always aware of the fact that God is the Lord of all creation and before His blessing all negative forces and satanic allurements must depart.

Exorcism

There are very serious and tough cases of satanic influence on certain individuals. This kind of effect is known as possession. Exorcism is the official prayer of the Church which can be conducted only by the priest who has been officially chosen by a bishop in order to deliver the possessed. However, the right diagnosis should be made to identify whether it is a real case of satanic influence, disturbances, or the real presence of the Evil One in a certain individual.

The Roman Ritual identifies three symptoms of possession: speaking in unknown languages, possessing superhuman strength and knowledge of hidden things.

The majority of exorcists claim that there are few cases of classical possession. The following is a real case told by an exorcist. The story involves a family of five; a married couple with three children. The husband is a doctor who previously had been very religious but he left the Church for ten years. The wife's father had been living for twenty-five years with his personal secretary, who had been a member of a Satanic sect that held black masses. The doctor's wife had never been a practising believer. One Ash Wednesday she went to church and came out with her eyes swollen and sore, and her face covered with blotches.

At the same time in their renovated and beautifully-decorated house, strange phenomena began to occur. They would find baking paper, ice cream and similar things on top of their closets and other high furniture, as well as on the shelves, which were impossible for their children to reach. The floor of the house was lifted up several times, even the upper floors. In rooms the walls would suddenly crack with water gushing out and then the cracks would close. Electrical appliances would often be out of order. They would call for an electrician who would find that the appliances were functioning normally. Immediately after the electrician left the house, the appliances would be out of order again. The family would normally open the electric fence when leaving the house in the morning, but it was impossible for them to close it again, so the fence would stay open throughout the day. In the evening they would be able to close the fence as usual. In the bottom of the closets they would find their clothes thrown down from hangers and on the inside walls of the closets they would find drops of blood. During the day and at night they could all occasionally hear heavy or light footsteps, and other types of sounds as if somebody was pulling paper across the floor or rolling ping-pong or pool balls. Their phone would call the numbers by itself. Suddenly the TV would turn on and off and the heating would turn on by itself, even in the summertime. It would turn on in the morning and off in the evening so that the house would be unbearably warm. The problems seemed insurmountable.

On top of it all, the husband and wife would often hear voices, even conversations of their children and cousins when they were not even around. At night their youngest son, a four-year-old child, would often cry, scream, beat and push his mother shouting: "I don't want you, I want my mummy!" This happened frequently. Several times they found balls of human excrement among the children's toys. They would clean everything in the evening, and then in the morning the excrement would reappear. The couple would fight without any reason whatsoever. The oldest child refused to go to church.

The list and variety of strange phenomena that exorcists usually come across in their practice is long. The mother in the story had strong temptations to commit suicide, especially while she was driving her car. She became convinced that the only logical conclusion was to pull off the road and kill herself.

The woman went to see a priest who did not have permission to pray the Rite of Exorcism. Her condition continued to deteriorate. Finally, she came upon the appointed exorcist. As soon as he uttered the words: "In the name of the Father" she fell into a trance, stretched down on the floor as if she was dead, grinning, trying to throw up, her eyeballs turned up so that only the whites of the eyes could be seen. Four persons were assisting the exorcist while she was having violent tantrums. She was shouting, whistling, and rejecting the exorcised water. When the exorcist put his hand on her belly it swelled and hardened, as if there was a fist-sized ball inside her that was moving. The exorcist demanded that the evil spirit say his name. The woman was trying to pronounce the name but was not able to say it. After a while she started to roll and writhe on the floor; she hurled a strong man who was holding her foot to the floor. At last they could hear the common evil spirit's statements such as: "I'm not going...She is mine." After more than an hour of prayer she regained her senses, a recovery of which was supported by prayers to Mother Mary.

The exorcist taught her how to use sacramentals for herself and her family (exorcised water, salt and oil), and he gave a warning to the whole family to return to prayer and the Christian way of living. The exorcist who shared his case with us is convinced that many disturbances that occurred in the aforementioned case originated from the wife, the husband, and his father-in-law who was living a disordered life. The exorcist is also convinced that after the prayer of exorcism, the family has been set on the right track. That is just one of many cases that exorcists come across in their practice.

In performing the rite of exorcism, the first prerequisite is faith on the part of the exorcist as well as faith on the part of the one who is being prayed over. Prayers of family members are very useful, too. It is highly recommended to ask a religious community of cloistered nuns and the whole parish or a particular prayer group to pray for the afflicted one. While performing the Rite of Exorcism, the use of appropriate sacramentals is helpful: blessed water, oil and salt. The rosary is of immense importance and the Word of God is extraordinarily effective. The exorcist must be a humble person, conducting a life of intense prayer and fasting. Nonetheless, the exorcist is only a man whom we should help with our prayers and sacrifices. He himself has to constantly struggle against Satan and his influence. For Satan takes revenge on the exorcist by using various schemes because the afflicted are set free from the bondage of demonic possession through the prayer of exorcism.

We should be aware of the fact that when an exorcist is praying the exorcism over a possessed person, it is Christ Himself who, through His Church, performs an exorcism: namely, the holy minister is performing it in the Name of Jesus who said: *"They will use my name to expel demons."* (Mk. 16:17) The Church is always acting in the Name of Jesus ('in persona Christi'). Therefore, the power resides in the Name of Jesus. Throughout history, the apostles and many saints cured the sick, resurrected the dead and drove out demons in His Name. The Name of Jesus is the most powerful force that the Church possesses in order to be always victorious against 'the powers of darkness.'

The Church has never stopped reminding the faithful of the necessity to stand up against Satan. Christians are 'in the world, but they do not belong to this world.' (cf. Jn. 17:11,14,16) On the contrary, they belong to Christ who redeemed them from the bondage of Satan. Concerning all that has been already mentioned, we should keep before our eyes the words of St. Paul, preparing us for the upcoming spiritual warfare: *"Finally, draw your strength from the Lord and his mighty power. Put on the armor of God so that you may be able to stand firm against the tactics of the devil. Our battle is not against human forces but against the principalities, with the powers, the rulers of this world of darkness, the evil spirits in regions above. You must put on the armor of God if you are to resist on the evil day; do all that your duty requires, and hold your ground. Stand fast, with the truth as a belt around your waist, justice as your breastplate, and zeal to propagate the gospel of peace as your footgear.*

In all circumstances hold faith up before you as your shield; it will help you extinguish the fiery darts of the evil one. Take the helmet of salvation and the sword of the spirit, the word of God. At every opportunity pray in the Spirit, using prayers and petitions of every sort. Pray constantly and attentively for all in the holy company..." (Eph. 6:10-18)

Every diocese should have an appointed exorcist but too many do not. One exorcist wisely remarked on one occasion that the devil never gives up in carrying out his duties while at the same time the servants of God are asleep, just as it is described in the parable of the good seed and the bad seed. It is urgent to educate the Catholic laity about this problem which has become more relevant and which is based on sound doctrine that is transmitted to us through Holy Scripture, Tradition, the Magisterium, and especially through the previous popes.

The ministers of Christ, the priests, exercise an extremely responsible function in the ministry of the Church. Monsignor Andrea Gemma, bishop of Isernia-Venafro (Italy), in his pastoral letter from June 29th of

1992, thus urges his priests: "I believe that part of the priestly service is to listen to all fellowmen with excessively great patience. All action should be subjected to the healthy discernment of spirits, especially on the part of the shepherds of the Church; isn't this their task anyway? They should never treat an afflicted soul in a superficial way, minimizing the problem of the afflicted one who may be unconscious of being tormented by the Evil One, or refusing to hear the person out, that would be even worse. Jesus did not treat people this way! Aren't the holy ministers aware that their very indifference towards people often forces simple and uninformed faithful to turn to soothsayers and witches or other fallacious practices which are, alas, the Devil's advantageous means for his action and victory? Do not ever get tired of keeping your faithful as far away as possible from those people."

Satan does not seem to encounter any barriers in his way and works ferociously using his vile influence to harm the souls and bodies of the faithful. One of the most crucial duties of priests is to demolish the malicious works of Satan, using all means available to limit Satan's liberty and suppress him in all possible ways. What is the worth of the power bestowed on priests if they don't use it for the purpose for which it has been given?

Certain individuals in the Church are endowed with special gifts — charisms — granted by the Lord to glorify Him and for the salvation of souls. Some have a special gift — the charism of deliverance from the devil's influence or presence, which is a rare gift. Some are given the charism of discernment of the spirits. Whoever receives such charisms has the right and duty to use them. It is up to the bishop to verify the authenticity of the gift with such individuals and determine their service in the Church.

Those individuals can surely be recognized by their fervor in prayer, their faith and their love; by their composed temperament and by prayers that are ingrained in the word of God and used in Church; their gratuitous care for the afflicted — *"The gift you have received, give as a gift;"* (Mt. 10:8) by their humility. (Whoever asserts to possess a particular charism, we can be sure that person does not have it.) *"You will know them by their deeds."* (Mt. 7:16)

Conclusion

People do not detect the wide scope of Satan's snares and evil activities. Therefore, many people unconsciously fall prey to occult practices out of curiosity or fashion as well as by the desire to ease their distressing physical or mental condition.

We should emphasize at this point that a crisis of faith generates darkness in which the objects of the living environment are not clearly visible. A crisis of faith comes from a deficiency of inner life, without which there is no creative activity whatsoever. Whoever does not live in grace cannot accomplish anything good.

Being aware of these facts and coming into contact with people who ask for assistance, I felt inspired through my long period of pastoral work to believe that something concrete ought to be done in regard to more thorough instruction of faithful adults. I began to conduct spiritual retreats for all age groups in many parishes within my archdiocese as well throughout the parishes of my country. I have held several spiritual retreats for the Croatian diaspora in the United States, Australia, Canada and several European countries. I have noticed how people show an earnest willingness to participate in spiritual renewals. The manner in which the retreats are conducted is easily acceptable for many. Many have experienced personal conversion of hearts and deliverance from numerous traumas and emotional wounds, their lives were changed and took on a new course for their future.

In an interview which was broadcast on radio for the Croatian diaspora in Windsor, Canada, I described the structure of such spiritual retreats, their topics and the way in which people are being delivered from the snares of the Evil One. The interview is recorded at the end of the book as a proposal and incentive for the pastoral work in our parishes.

I hope that the content of this book has revealed important insights into a new life of conversion and faith and that you would not let your life be a house built on sand but founded on the solid rock. To achieve this, do not stop; do away with all inclinations towards idols of every kind.

I urge you to dedicate and yield your spiritual and earthly life, everything you have and who you are to the Sacred Heart of Jesus and to the Immaculate Heart of Mary. Our abode and peace are in the love of the most Sacred Heart of Our Lord, who redeemed us with His Blood, and no one will ever advocate for us more earnestly with a holy love and humility than the Immaculate Heart of Mother Mary.

So surrender yourself, with trust of a child, to these Sacred Hearts. Do the devotion of the nine First Fridays (every first Friday of the month you should confess and receive communion).

You will attain peace for your soul and you will grow on the path of holiness for the joy of our Father who is in heaven.

Don Milivoj Bolobanic

Interview on Spiritual Retreat

The interview was conducted by Gracia Kutlesa,
Croatian Parish of St. Francis of Assisi,
Windsor, Canada

Could you explain briefly what a spiritual retreat is and who needs it?

Basically, a spiritual retreat means the evangelization of adults. It means leading an adult believer on the path of conversion, to the conscious and responsible embracement of baptism, or helping an adult to make a fundamental change in his life and irrevocably choose Jesus Christ, who will become his only Way, the Truth and the Life. The Holy Father believes that such spiritual retreats are necessary for all adult faithful in the Church as many of them have not had the opportunity to encounter Jesus Christ personally, as mature people, and make this final decision. Namely, they have never had an encounter with the living God.

There is a growing number of the faithful, torn by religious doubts, who do not see any meaning in their lives, similar to wanderers in the wastelands searching for the right path. Their lives have become monotonous and boring, they are embittered and deeply afflicted or dejected, sluggish and frustrated; they carry internal traumas and barriers; they may have strong addictions of some kind. They may be enslaved by sin and long for deliverance; they are oppressed by numerous hardships. To all those suffering out there, whom we can all easily identify or recognize in one way or another, I want to say that every adult person needs a spiritual retreat.

What is the method or the manner that you have chosen to conduct this spiritual retreat in order to realize everything you have spoken about?

First of all, I have chosen some basic themes which I believe are fundamental and essential for intensifying one's faith and making it

100

personal. For this purpose, and keeping these themes in mind, I prepared the talks and tried to mold them in a form of representation that would be simple, comprehensible and acceptable to all. Secondly, I think that the most important part of a spiritual retreat is meditative prayer, creating the possibility for each participant to encounter personally the living God, Jesus Christ. For wonderful things happen in this personal encounter where the Holy Spirit operates in a special way. He is an invisible but real agent, who makes it possible for each sincere and well-disposed participant to personally experience the living God so that, illuminated by God's light, one can penetrate deeper into one's being and become aware of the inner state of one's soul, of all positive and negative experiences, of desires and yearnings, fears and discontentment, faith and lack of faith. When a person comes to know the inner condition of his own soul and entirely accepts himself for who he is, then he can, with God's assistance, experience more intimately and personally his faith. The talks serve as a means of expounding certain truths. In my opinion, the step that is most important in a spiritual retreat is meditative prayer which brings him to a personal conversion.

Could you tell us briefly something about the main themes that you have chosen for the spiritual retreat?

The first theme I expounded on was sin as a mystery of evil in the world and in life. I think of sin as the crux of the problem, the point we all should start from. Every person feels and carries a profound experience of evil inside oneself. We all know that we ought to do good and yet we do evil. Where did this stalking curse come from? The Bible gives us the answer. Breaking up the relationship with God happened at the dawn of human history. Man broke off his ties with his Source. The evil spirit, Satan, seduced man, and man, by submitting to seduction, gave Satan dominion over the world that God the Creator had given to man. Since then, sin arouses feelings of guilt and fear in men; man becomes a slave to sin. In a very cunning way Satan keeps tempting man to do evil works, which all of us have experienced in our lifetime. Wickedness has crept into the hearts of men, poisoning them to the core. Satan is stronger than man and man cannot resist him on his own.

Is there a way out of this sinister and grim situation?

Only the Bible gives us the answer about the origin of evil and the ways in which we can liberate ourselves from it. Sin produced fear in man and an overall loss of confidence in God. The only one in human history who trusted God all the way, wholly and perfectly, was Jesus Christ of Nazareth. Faithful to His Father, He died with the certainty that God the Father would not abandon Him at death. Thus Jesus' resurrection is the powerful proof that God loves and delivers man from all evil, even death, provided man remains faithful till the end.

Therefore, my second theme was Jesus Christ and redemption. I tried to present Jesus as the most prominent Teacher of all times and not just someone whose talks were wondrous. He did much more than this; He showed in His deeds that He is mightier than evil, Satan and death itself. Jesus loved us: wretched, misled and sinful people, and out of love for His Heavenly Father and through His death on the cross, Jesus redeemed man from the power of sin, opening the way to freedom and to a new life in all its fullness. Jesus Christ of Nazareth is the irrefutable proof of how much God loves man. God loves us because He is all goodness and not because we are good. He asks nothing from us except that we allow Him to lavish His love on us and to save us.

You have said that Jesus Christ is the only Savior and Redeemer of man. But how can poor and sinful man come to Jesus Christ and receive all that He has achieved for us?

The question is logical. Jesus Christ Himself gives us the answer: "Repent, and believe in the Gospel." Hence, there are two steps by which we can attain all that Jesus has promised, fulfilled and done for us: conversion and faith. That is why the talk for the next spiritual retreat had the title: "Conversion as the fundamental choice for man."

In this talk I explain that conversion means abandoning the vain attempts of trying to rule our own lives and, instead, submitting completely to God so that He can rule our lives. This means giving ourselves wholly to God or, in other words, God should occupy the first place in our lives and we should finally do away with the mistrust in God which we have fostered in our hearts. Basically, one must see through the true nature of Satan and unmask his evil allurement by which he enticingly misleads and lies to us, promising now this or that success that in reality just attracts and destroys man, his life and happiness. Therefore, to convert means to put an end to every conscious cooperation with Satan and with all that he has to offer. Let us put God in the first place. Let God be the first and the most important person in our lives so that we will not be slaves to evil and sin but, on the contrary, that we can have life in all its fullness. Man's life has only two basic possibilities: life or death. To convert means to choose life!

What you have said is true but it is not an easy thing to do. I would even say that it may be impossible for man to do. How can this be achieved in one's life?

102

Your observation is very accurate when you say that this goes way beyond man's power and ability. Faith is needed. Faith is essential for the normal functioning of man and for opening him up to future events. Faith is needed as well so that man can abandon himself entirely to God, that is, to convert. So one of the following themes at the retreat is "Faith as a way out from death and sin in the life of man" where I try to show what real faith means in the life of man. It is not merely a belief that there is God, or being convinced that Sacred Scripture contains something that God has said. Faith means much more than that. Believing means having confidence in God, making Him a stronghold to lean on, putting yourself in God's hands, surrendering your life to Jesus Christ. Let Him guide your life, lean on God even when it looks like everything around you is falling apart. Have faith that you will live even when you see you are dying, have faith even when it looks like you are losing everything.

However, even faith is not something that man can attain and realize with his own strength and ability.

Faith is primarily a gift from God. It is a gift of the Holy Spirit. And being a gift it cannot be bought or extorted. God gives it freely, out of goodness and generosity. And He gives it to those who want it, who are open to this gift. That is why we say that this gift can be obtained through prayer, which was another theme of spiritual renewal: 'Prayer as permanent companionship and continuing encounter with God.' First we try to understand how prayer is a conversation with God. We need to have two parties involved if we want to converse: man and God. That is why prayer is not a monologue to God but for us it is first and foremost the listening and hearing of God's words. In order for man to hear God's words he must be composed and concentrated, which means being conscious of himself, being at home with himself. Thus, during our spiritual retreat we have tried to train ourselves to keep a composed and collected presence of mind so that all participants might be able to hear God's words. Through meditative and spontaneous prayer, God strengthens and fortifies the faith of all who participate in the spiritual retreat. In addition to a composed presence of mind, another precondition was requested from the participants for successful prayer, which was their willingness to forgive all those against whom they held a grudge against. Hatred, enmity and vengeance are often great obstacles inside us, preventing our prayers from being answered. In each prayer we should be asking for God's will to be done. God knows best what is good for us. Jesus Himself taught us that in prayer we should seek first the Kingdom of God and then everything else will be given to us. One learns to pray only by praying every day with perseverance and patience so that God may keep molding us ceaselessly for the better through our prayer. To put it simply, to pray means to live.

Everything that you have told us so far is wonderful and it represents an ideal which every man should strive to fulfill. Now I would like to ask you an intriguing question: has anything that you have told us become real in the lives of those who participated in the spiritual retreat?

Indeed, these would just be sweet words and vain promises if nothing of what we did at this retreat became a reality. After presenting all the talks and our collective reflections, the participants become firmly convinced that this world is in God's hand, that all the power in the world and all creation has been handed over to Jesus Christ. He is the only power of the world that can resolve all our heartaches. Finally, when all the essential reflective points have been grasped, each participant has to face head on the fundamental decision of his life and make a choice: Jesus Christ or Satan. There is no other option. Hence, a fundamental choice has to be made. After conversations I had with several participants and after hearing their confessions, I deeply believed that many took this retreat very seriously and turned irrevocably and with intense resolution to Jesus Christ, choosing Him to be their leader and teacher.

Probably something else had to be done beyond this fundamental decision making?

The next step was to banish firmly from one's life all idols or false gods that people thought to be more important than the true God. Furthermore, the participants had to be instructed, by all means, to see and perceive what or who were for them false gods in their own lives. The false god can be a person who enslaves another person, or it can be one's work, an object or a hazardous practice. On the other hand, a person can be influenced by evil or demonic forces. Contemporary man is often impelled by alluring offers and TV commercials, radio and magazines that have made him become more and more interested in literature from the domains of mystery and the occult. As a result, he eagerly reads the horoscope, desirous to learn something about his future; he has a penchant for divination by coffee grains, tea leaves, cards, a pendulum, palm reading or any other way of divination, in hopes of having a glimpse into future events. Many engage themselves in various magic practices and read the existing literature that introduces them to the mysterious workings of black and white magic. Some people tend toward invoking the spirits of the dead, so-called spiritism.

New sects are swelling their ranks with more and more followers, distributing books and magazines, in particular the religions from the East like Hare Krishna, Zen Buddhism and transcendental meditation.

In our present day we have the New Age movement along with various sinister sects, like satanic sects, where Christ is overtly rejected and Satan is honored, to whom even human sacrifices are offered and blood pacts are signed. The number of people that randomly come into contact with these practices is growing. Many of them fall into some kind of lethargic state of mind, meditating on the meaninglessness of life. They are often assaulted with black thoughts, tempted to commit suicide, feel restless and have nightmares. They begin to hate themselves and others, are gripped by fears, feel the presence of other beings inside them, are unable to get rid of vices and are unable to concentrate while praying. They desire deliverance from all these negative assaults and look for help from whomever and wherever. In many cases they go to those who only entangle them deeper in evil activities — soothsayers, fortune-tellers, pseudo-healers, therapeutic touch healers, rod dowsers and similar individuals involved in the various occult practices — in other words, satanic practices and affairs. Unfortunately, people are mostly uninformed because no one has ever instructed them about this. As a result, they submit to this form of idolatry, paying homage to false gods.

We know what God says in His first commandment: "I am the Lord." Therefore, whoever is engaged in these practices, jumps unwarily into the territory of the evil spirit who, from that moment on, has some kind of joint ownership in his life, tormenting him in many ways. Occultism and everything related to it is a great obstacle for man embarking on the course of life in Jesus Christ, undisturbed and in great confidence. This is the reason why we requested the participants at the spiritual retreat to renounce Satan resolutely, to renounce all of his works that we have mentioned above, and to renounce all his dazzling false brightness with which he entices and seduces us. After this we pray the prayer of deliverance so that Jesus, who is the source of salvation for all people and is the same today as He was when He walked on earth, might save and deliver every participant at the retreat from all the negative effects of the evil spirits, through His divine power and through His Passion and Blood which He shed for us. People feel truly liberated afterwards.

What about the personal sins that the people consciously commit in their lives?

Certainly that needs to be discussed. That is the next step we followed in order to realize concrete deliverance and salvation of the participants at the retreat. Everyone, especially those who had never done a life confession, are given the opportunity of making a thorough confession of their whole life. This means to confess all the sins that the individual committed in his entire life, regardless of whether those sins had already been confessed and whether he had ever had the courage to confess them. I can say that many wonderful and sincere confessions were done, after which people felt renewed, pure and restored, at peace with God and their brothers and sisters, reassured that now they could start to live a pure life, unburdened by the past.

People are burdened by their different psychological traumas and wounds a reminder of all the negative things that occurred in their lives. And they suffer for this. Did anything happen in this respect as well?

Sometimes even after having made a good confession a man experiences some sort of inability to have earnest and thorough faith, and feels as if he is being torn from within, feels some wounds or sores and scars in his soul. The origin and root of these conditions are often unknown and hidden in his subconscious mind, from where they govern many of man's actions towards other people and God, leaving man unconscious to that fact. We have inherited many things from our ancestors or some traumas happened to us in early childhood and we lost memory of that. Jesus came to save man in his entirety. Therefore, we believe that the Lord wants to heal and free us from all our scars and wounds that we carry within us. At the end of the retreat program we prayed a very important prayer for this purpose that is called: "Prayer for inner healing." This prayer is the last step in the practical implementation of our deliverance. By listening to the testimonies of the participants, one could clearly see on their faces that the Lord was truly present as well as very active in the lives of all those who had opened their hearts to Him in faith.

Prayers for Spiritual and Physical Healing

Sign of the Cross

In the name of the Father, and the Son, and the Holy Spirit. Amen.

Our Father

Our Father, who art in heaven, hallowed be thy name; thy kingdom come; thy will be done on earth as it is in heaven. Give us this day our daily bread; and forgive us our trespasses as we forgive those who trespass against us; and lead us not into temptation, but deliver us from evil. Amen.

Hail Mary

Hail Mary, full of grace, the Lord is with thee. Blessed art thou among women and blessed is the fruit of thy womb, Jesus.

Holy Mary, Mother of God, pray for us sinners, now and at the hour of our death. Amen.

Glory Be

Glory be to the Father, and to the Son, and to the Holy Spirit. As it was in the beginning, is now, and ever shall be, world without end. Amen.

Apostles' Creed

I believe in God, the Father almighty, Creator of heaven and earth, and in Jesus Christ, his only Son, our Lord, who was conceived by the Holy Spirit, born of the Virgin Mary, suffered under Pontius Pilate, was crucified, died and was buried; he descended into hell; on the third day he rose again from the dead; he ascended into heaven, and is seated at the right hand of God the Father almighty; from there he will come to judge the living and the dead. I believe in the Holy Spirit, the holy catholic Church, the communion of saints, the forgiveness of sins, the resurrection of the body, and life everlasting. Amen.

Angelus

The angel of the Lord declared unto Mary,
And she conceived of the Holy Spirit. Hail Mary...
Behold, the handmaid of the Lord;
Be it done to me according to your word. Hail Mary...
And the Word was made Flesh,
And dwelt among us. Hail Mary...
Pray for us, O holy Mother of God;
That we may be made worthy of the promises of Christ.

Let us pray, Pour forth, we beseech you, O Lord, Your grace into our hearts that we, to whom the Incarnation of Christ, Your Son, was made known by the message of an angel, may by His Passion and Cross be brought to the glory of His Resurrection. Through the same Christ, our Lord. Amen.

Regina Caeli (Queen of Heaven)

It is sung in standing position in place of the Angelus during the Easter season, from Holy Saturday to the Feast of the Most Holy Trinity.

Queen of Heaven, rejoice, alleluia!
Whom you did merit to bear, alleluia!
Has risen as He said, alleluia!
Pray for us to God, alleluia!
Rejoice and be glad, O Virgin Mary, alleluia!
For the Lord has truly risen, alleluia!

Let us pray, O God, who gave joy to the world through the resurrection of Thy Son, our Lord Jesus Christ, grant we beseech you, that through the intercession of the Virgin Mary, his mother, we may attain the joys of everlasting life, through the same Christ our Lord. Amen.

Regina Caeli, laetare, alleluia
Quia quem meruisti portare, alleluia.
Resurrexit, sicut dixit, alleluia.
Ora pro nobis Deum, alleluia.
Gaude et laetare, Virgo Maria, alleluia.
Quia surrexit Dominus vere, alleluia.

Oremus, Deus, qui per resurrectionem Filii tui, Domini nostri Iesu Christi, mundum laetificare dignatus es: praesta, quaesumus; ut per eius Genetricem Virginem Mariam, perpetuae capiamus gaudia vitae. Per eundem Christum Dominum nostrum. Amen.

Rosary of the Blessed Virgin Mary

Make the Sign of the Cross and then say:

O Jesus, this is for love of You, for the conversion of sinners and for the sins committed against the Immaculate Heart of Mary.

Holding the cross of the rosary pray the Apostles' Creed:

I believe in God, the Father almighty, Creator of heaven and earth, and in Jesus Christ, his only Son, our Lord, who was conceived by the Holy Spirit, born of the Virgin Mary, suffered under Pontius Pilate, was crucified, died and was buried; he descended into hell; on the third day he rose again from the dead; he ascended into heaven, and is seated at the right hand of God the Father almighty; from there he will come to judge the living and the dead. I believe in the Holy Spirit, the holy catholic Church, the communion of saints, the forgiveness of sins, the resurrection of the body, and life everlasting. Amen.

Then on the large bead pray the Our Father followed by three Hail Marys on the three small beads. After the word 'Jesus' pray:

Who may increase our faith!

Who may strengthen our hope!

Who may perfect our love!

Then pray the Glory be to the Father followed by the Fatima Prayer: "O my Jesus, forgive us our sins, save us from the fires of hell, lead all souls to heaven, especially those who are in most need of Thy mercy."

After each decade pray:

Glory be to the Father... and the Fatima Prayer

THE JOYFUL MYSTERIES

(On Mondays and Saturdays)
The Annunciation
The Visitation
The Nativity
The Presentation in the Temple
The Finding in the Temple

THE LUMINOUS MYSTERIES

(On Thursdays)
The Baptism in the Jordan
The Wedding at Cana

The Proclamation of the Kingdom
The Transfiguration
The Institution of the Eucharist

THE SORROWFUL MYSTERIES

(On Tuesdays and Fridays)
The Agony in the Garden
The Scourging at the Pillar
The Crowning with Thorns
The Carrying of the Cross
The Crucifixion

THE GLORIOUS MYSTERIES

(On Wednesdays and Sundays)
The Resurrection
The Ascension
The Descent of the Holy Spirit
The Assumption
The Coronation of the Blessed Virgin Mary

Each mystery of the Rosary can also be prayed meditating on a passage from Scripture like this:
In the Name of the Father...
O God, come to my assistance.
O Lord, make haste to help me.
Glory be to the Father, and to the Son, and to the Holy Spirit...

THE JOYFUL MYSTERIES

In the First Joyful Mystery, let us meditate on how the Archangel Gabriel announced to the Blessed Virgin Mary that she will conceive by the power of the Holy Spirit and give birth to the Son of God.

1 Our Father... 10 Hail Marys... 1 Glory be...

In the Second Joyful Mystery, let us meditate on how the Blessed Virgin Mary visited her cousin, St. Elizabeth and spent three months in her home.

1 Our Father... 10 Hail Marys... 1 Glory be...

In the Third Joyful Mystery, let us meditate on how the Blessed Virgin Mary gave birth to our Lord Jesus Christ in a cave in Bethlehem and placed Him in a manger.

1 Our Father... 10 Hail Marys... 1 Glory be...

In the Fourth Joyful Mystery, let us meditate on how the Blessed Virgin Mary, forty days after giving birth, brought her Son to the temple to present Him to the heavenly Father. There Simeon, an old man, took Him in his arms and blessed God.

1 Our Father... 10 Hail Marys... 1 Glory be...

In the Fifth Joyful Mystery, let us meditate on how the Blessed Virgin Mary found her twelve-year-old Son in the temple talking with the teachers.

1 Our Father... 10 Hail Marys... 1 Glory be....

THE LUMINOUS MYSTERIES

In the First Luminous Mystery, let us meditate on how, during the baptism of Our Lord Jesus Christ in the Jordan, the Holy Spirit descended upon Him and the Father declared Him to be His beloved Son.

1 Our Father... 10 Hail Marys... 1 Glory be...

In the Second Luminous Mystery, let us meditate on how Jesus Christ, Our Lord, through the intervention of Mary, changed the water into wine at the wedding in Cana and thus opened the hearts of the disciples to faith.

1 Our Father...10 Hail Marys... 1 Glory be...

In the Third Luminous Mystery, let us meditate on how Jesus Christ, Our Lord, proclaimed the coming of the Kingdom of God and called to conversion and forgiveness of sins of all who draw near to Him in humble trust.

1 Our Father... 10 Hail Marys...1 Glory be...

In the Fourth Luminous Mystery, let us meditate on how Jesus Christ, Our Lord, to whom God the Father called us to listen when He was transfigured before His disciples on Mount Tabor.

1 Our Father...10 Hail Marys...1 Glory be...

In the Fifth Luminous Mystery, let us meditate on how Jesus Christ, Our Lord, instituted the Eucharist with which He feeds us with His Body and Blood under the form of bread and wine.

1 Our Father...10 Hail Marys...1 Glory be...

THE SORROWFUL MYSTERIES

In the First Sorrowful Mystery, let us meditate on how Our Lord Jesus Christ prayed to His Heavenly Father and sweat blood in the Garden of Gethsemane.

1 Our Father... 10 Hail Marys... 1 Glory be...

In the Second Sorrowful Mystery, let us meditate on how Our Lord Jesus Christ was tied to a stone pillar and bitterly scourged in Pilate's court.

1 Our Father... 10 Hail Marys... 1 Glory be...

In the Third Sorrowful Mystery, let us meditate on how Our Lord Jesus Christ was crowned with thorns.

1 Our Father... 10 Hail Marys... 1 Glory be...

In the Fourth Sorrowful Mystery, let us meditate on how Our Lord Jesus Christ was condemned to death and how He carried the heavy cross up to Calvary.

1 Our Father... 10 Hail Marys... 1 Glory be...

In the Fifth Sorrowful Mystery, let us meditate on how Our Lord Jesus Christ was crucified between two criminals and how His sorrowful Mother stood by the cross.

1 Our Father... 10 Hail Marys... 1 Glory be...

THE GLORIOUS MYSTERIES

In the First Glorious Mystery, let us meditate on how Our Lord Jesus Christ rose from the dead on the third day after His passion and death, never to die again.

1 Our Father... 10 Hail Marys... 1 Glory be...

In the Second Glorious Mystery, let us meditate on how Our Lord Jesus Christ, forty days after His resurrection, ascended into heaven and sits at the right hand of God the Father.

1 Our Father... 10 Hail Marys... 1 Glory be...

In the Third Glorious Mystery, let us meditate on how Our Lord Jesus Christ sent the Holy Spirit to His apostles in the form of fiery tongues.

1 Our Father... 10 Hail Marys... 1 Glory be...

In the Fourth Glorious Mystery, let us meditate on how the Blessed Virgin Mary passed away from this world and was assumed body and soul into heaven.

1 Our Father... 10 Hail Marys... 1 Glory be...

In the Fifth Glorious Mystery, let us meditate on how the Most Holy Trinity crowned the Blessed Virgin Mary, Queen of Heaven and Earth, and let us also reflect on the heavenly bliss of all the Saints.

1 Our Father... 10 Hail Marys... 1 Glory be...

Hail, Holy Queen, Mother of Mercy, our life, our sweetness and our hope, to thee do we cry, poor banished children of Eve; to thee do we send up our sighs, mourning and weeping in this vale of tears; turn, then, most gracious Advocate, thine eyes of mercy toward us, and after this, our exile, show unto us the blessed fruit of thy womb, Jesus. O clement, O loving, O sweet Virgin Mary!

Pray for us, O holy Mother of God, that we may be made worthy of the promises of Christ. Amen.

Let us pray. O God, whose only-begotten Son by his life, death and resurrection has purchased for us the rewards of eternal life, grant, we beseech you, that by meditating on these mysteries of the most holy rosary of the Blessed Virgin Mary, we may imitate what they contain and obtain what they promise. Through the same Christ, Our Lord. Amen.

Litany of the Blessed Virgin Mary, the Mother of God

Lord, have mercy on us.
Christ, have mercy on us.
Lord, have mercy on us. Christ, hear us.
Christ, graciously hear us.
God the Father of heaven, *have mercy on us.*
God the Son, Redeemer of the world, *have mercy on us.*
God the Holy Spirit, *have mercy on us.*
Holy Trinity, one God, *have mercy on us.*
Holy Mary, *pray for us.*
Holy Mother of God, *etc.*
Holy Virgin of Virgins,
Mother of Christ,
Mother of divine grace,
Mother most pure,
Mother most chaste,
Mother inviolate,
Mother undefiled,
Mother most amiable,
Mother most admirable,
Mother of good counsel,
Mother of our Creator,
Mother of our Savior,
Mother of the Church,
Virgin most prudent,

Virgin most venerable,
Virgin most renowned,
Virgin most powerful,
Virgin most merciful,
Virgin most faithful,
Mirror of justice,
Seat of wisdom,
Cause of our joy,
Spiritual vessel,
Vessel of honor,
Singular vessel of devotion,
Mystical rose,
Tower of David,
Tower of ivory,
House of gold,
Ark of the covenant,
Gate of heaven,
Morning star,
Health of the sick,
Refuge of sinners,
Comforter of the afflicted,
Help of Christians,
Queen of angels,
Queen of patriarchs,
Queen of prophets,
Queen of apostles,
Queen of martyrs,
Queen of confessors,
Queen of virgins,
Queen of all saints,
Queen conceived without original sin,
Queen assumed into heaven,
Queen of the most holy rosary,
Queen of families,
Queen of peace.

Lamb of God, who takes away the sins of the world,
Spare us, O Lord.

Lamb of God, who takes away the sins of the world,
Graciously hear us, O Lord.
Lamb of God, who takes away the sins of the world,
Have mercy on us.
Pray for us, O holy Mother of God.
That we may be made worthy of the promises of Christ.

Let us pray. Grant we beseech Thee, O Lord God, that we Thy servants may enjoy perpetual health of mind and body and by the glorious intercession of the Blessed Mary, ever Virgin, be delivered from the present sorrow and enjoy eternal happiness. Through Christ Our Lord. Amen.

Litany to the Holy Trinity

Lord, have mercy.
Lord, have mercy.
Christ, have mercy.
Christ, have mercy.
Lord, have mercy.
Lord, have mercy.
Blessed Trinity, *hear us.*
Adorable Unity, *graciously hear us.*
God the Father of Heaven, *Have mercy on us.*
God the Son, Redeemer of the world, *etc.*
God the Holy Ghost,
Holy Trinity, One God,
Father from Whom are all things,
Son through Whom are all things,
Holy Ghost in Whom are all things,
Holy and undivided Trinity,
Father everlasting,
Only-begotten Son of the Father,
Spirit Who proceedeth from the Father and the Son,
Co-eternal Majesty of Three Divine Persons,
Father, the Creator,
Son, the Redeemer,
Holy Ghost, the Comforter,
Holy, holy, holy, Lord God of hosts,
Who art, Who wast, and Who art to come,

God Most High, Who inhabitest eternity,
To Whom alone are due all honor and glory,
Who alone doest great wonders,
Power infinite,
Wisdom, incomprehensible,
Love unspeakable, *be merciful,*
Spare us, O Holy Trinity,
Graciously hear us, O Holy Trinity.
From all evil, *deliver us, O Holy Trinity.*
From all sin, *etc.*
From all pride,
From all love of riches,
From all uncleanness,
From all sloth,
From all inordinate affection,
From all envy and malice,
From all anger and impatience,
From every thought, word, and deed contrary to Thy holy law,
From Thine everlasting malediction,
Through Thine almighty power,
Through Thy plenteous loving kindness,
Through the exceeding treasure of Thy goodness and love,
Through the depths of Thy wisdom and knowledge,
Through all Thy unspeakable perfections,
We sinners, beseech Thee, hear us.
That we may ever serve Thee alone, *we beseech Thee, hear us.*
That we may worship Thee in spirit and in truth, *etc.*
That we may love Thee with all our heart, with all our soul, and
with all our strength,
That, for Thy sake, we may love our neighbor as ourselves,
That we may faithfully keep Thy holy commandments,
That we may never defile our bodies and souls with sin,
That we may go from grace to grace, and from virtue to virtue,
That we may finally enjoy the sight of Thee in glory,
That Thou wouldst vouchsafe to hear us,
O Blessed Trinity,
We beseech Thee, deliver us.
O Blessed Trinity,

We beseech Thee, save us.
O Blessed Trinity,
Have mercy on us.
Lord, have mercy,
Lord, have mercy.
Christ, have mercy,
Christ, have mercy.
Lord, have mercy,
Lord, have mercy.
Our Father... Hail Mary...
Blessed art Thou, O Lord, in the firmament of Heaven,
And worthy to be praised, and glorious, and highly exalted forever.

Let us pray, Almighty and everlasting God, Who hast granted Thy servants in the confession of the True Faith to acknowledge the glory of an Eternal Trinity, and in the power of Thy majesty to adore Thy Unity: we beseech Thee that by the strength of this faith we may be defended from all adversity. Through Jesus Christ Our Lord. Amen.

Litany of the Most Holy Name of Jesus

Lord, have mercy on us.
Christ have mercy on us.
Lord, have mercy on us. Jesus, hear us.
Jesus graciously hear us.
God, the Father of Heaven, *have mercy on us.*
God, the Son, Redeemer of the world, *etc.*
God, the Holy Spirit,
Holy Trinity, One God,
Jesus, Son of the living God,
Jesus, Splendor of the Father,
Jesus, Brightness of eternal Light,
Jesus, King of Glory,
Jesus, Sun of Justice,
Jesus, Son of the Virgin Mary,
Jesus, most amiable,
Jesus, most admirable,
Jesus, the mighty God,
Jesus, Father of the world to come,
Jesus, angel of great counsel,

Jesus, most powerful,
Jesus, most patient,
Jesus, most obedient,
Jesus, meek and humble of heart,
Jesus, Lover of Chastity,
Jesus, Lover of us,
Jesus, God of Peace,
Jesus, Author of Life,
Jesus, Model of Virtues,
Jesus, zealous for souls,
Jesus, our God,
Jesus, our Refuge,
Jesus, Father of the poor,
Jesus, Treasure of the faithful,
Jesus, good Shepherd,
Jesus, true Light,
Jesus, eternal Wisdom,
Jesus, infinite Goodness,
Jesus, our Way and our Life,
Jesus, joy of the Angels,
Jesus, King of the Patriarchs,
Jesus, Master of the Apostles,
Jesus, Teacher of the Evangelists,
Jesus, Strength of Martyrs,
Jesus, Light of Confessors,
Jesus, Purity of Virgins,
Jesus, Crown of all Saints,
Be merciful,
Spare us, O Jesus!
Be merciful,
Graciously hear us, O Jesus!
From all evil, *deliver us, O Jesus.*
From all sin, *etc.*
From Your wrath,
From the snares of the devil,
From the spirit of fornication,
From everlasting death,
From the neglect of Your inspirations,

Through the mystery of Your holy Incarnation,
Through Your Nativity,
Through Your Infancy,
Through Your most divine Life,
Through Your Labors,
Through Your Agony and Passion,
Through Your Cross and Dereliction,
Through Your Sufferings,
Through Your Death and Burial,
Through Your Resurrection,
Through Your Ascension,
Through Your Institution of the Most Holy Eucharist,
Through Your Joys,
Through Your Glory,
Lamb of God, who takes away the sins of the world,
Spare us, O Jesus!
Lamb of God, who takes away the sins of the world,
Graciously hear us, O Jesus!
Lamb of God, who takes away the sins of the world,
Have mercy on us, O Jesus!
Jesus, hear us.
Jesus, graciously hear us.

Let us pray. O Lord Jesus Christ, You have said, "Ask and you shall receive; seek, and you shall find; knock, and it shall be opened to you;" mercifully attend to our supplications, and grant us the grace of Your most divine love, that we may love You with all our hearts, and in all our words and actions, and never cease to praise You.

Make us, O Lord, to have both a perpetual fear and love of Your holy name, for You never fail to govern those whom You have solidly established in Your love. You, who live and reign forever and ever. Amen.

Chaplet of the Sacred Heart of Jesus (Golden Chaplet)

It is prayed on a regular rosary
After the Sign of the Cross pray:
Sweet Heart of my Jesus,
Make me love Thee ever more and more.
On large beads (instead of Our Father) pray:
Eternal Father, I offer you the infinite treasure of the Most Precious Blood of Jesus Christ in atonement for my sins and in supplication for the holy souls in Purgatory, and for the needs of the Holy Church.
On small beads (instead of Hail Mary) pray:
Jesus, meek and humble of Heart,
Make my heart like unto Thine.
Instead of Glory be to the Father...pray:
Sweet Heart of Mary,
Be my salvation!
At the end pray:
Our Father...Hail Mary...Glory be to the Father.

Litany of the Most Sacred Heart of Jesus

Lord, have mercy on us.
Christ, have mercy on us.
Lord, have mercy. Christ, hear us.
Christ, graciously hear us.
God, the Father of Heaven, *have mercy on us.*
God, the Son, Redeemer of the world, *etc.*
God, the Holy Spirit,
Holy Trinity, One God,
Heart of Jesus, Son of the Eternal Father.
Heart of Jesus, formed by the Holy Spirit in the womb of the Virgin Mother,
Heart of Jesus, substantially united to the Word of God,
Heart of Jesus, of infinite majesty,
Heart of Jesus, holy Temple of God,
Heart of Jesus, Tabernacle of the Most High,
Heart of Jesus, House of God and Gate of Heaven,
Heart of Jesus, burning Furnace of charity,
Heart of Jesus, Vessel of justice and love,

Heart of Jesus, full of goodness and love,
Heart of Jesus, Abyss of all virtues,
Heart of Jesus, most worthy of all praise,
Heart of Jesus, King and center of all hearts,
Heart of Jesus, in Whom are all the treasures of wisdom and knowledge,
Heart of Jesus, in Whom dwelleth all the fullness of the divinity,
Heart of Jesus, in Whom the Father was well pleased,
Heart of Jesus, of whose fullness we have all received,
Heart of Jesus, desire of the everlasting hills,
Heart of Jesus, patient and abounding in mercy,
Heart of Jesus, rich unto all who call upon Thee,
Heart of Jesus, Fountain of life and holiness,
Heart of Jesus, Propitiation for our sins,
Heart of Jesus, filled with reproaches,
Heart of Jesus, bruised for our offenses,
Heart of Jesus, made obedient to death,
Heart of Jesus, pierced with a lance,
Heart of Jesus, Source of all consolation,
Heart of Jesus, our Life and Resurrection,
Heart of Jesus, our Peace and Reconciliation,
Heart of Jesus, Victim for our sins,
Heart of Jesus, Salvation of those who hope in Thee,
Heart of Jesus, Hope of those who die in Thee,
Heart of Jesus, Delight of all the Saints,
Lamb of God, who takes away the sins of the world.
Spare us, O Lord.
Lamb of God, who takes away the sins of the world,
Graciously hear us, O Lord.
Lamb of God, who takes away the sins of the world,
Have mercy on us.
Jesus, meek and humble of heart.
Make our hearts like yours.

Let us pray. Almighty and eternal God, consider the Heart of Thy well-beloved Son and the praises and satisfaction He offers Thee in the name of sinners; appeased by worthy homage, pardon those who implore Thy mercy, in the name of the same Jesus Christ Thy Son, Who lives and reigns with Thee, world without end. Amen.

The Chaplet of Divine Mercy

It is prayed on regular rosary beads.
1. Begin with the Sign of the Cross, then pray one Our Father, Hail Mary,
and the Apostles' Creed.
2. On the large beads pray:
Eternal Father, I offer You the Body and Blood, Soul and Divinity
of Your dearly beloved Son, Our Lord Jesus Christ,
In atonement for our sins and those of the whole world.
3. On the small beads pray:
For the sake of His sorrowful Passion,
Have mercy on us and on the whole world.
(Repeat step 2 and 3 for all five decades).
4. Conclude with
Holy God, Holy Mighty One, Holy Immortal One, have mercy
on us and on the whole world. (3x)
O Blood and Water which gushed forth from the Heart of Jesus
as a fount of Mercy for us, I trust in You. (3x)
St. Faustina, Pray for us.

Litany of Divine Mercy

The Love of God is the flower — *Mercy the fruit.*
Let the doubting soul read these considerations on Divine Mercy
and become trusting.
Divine Mercy, gushing forth from the bosom of the Father,
I trust in You.
Divine Mercy, greatest attribute of God, *etc.*
Divine Mercy, incomprehensible mystery,
Divine Mercy, fount gushing forth from the mystery of the
Most Blessed Trinity,
Divine Mercy, unfathomed by any intellect, human or angelic,
Divine Mercy, from which wells forth all life and happiness,
Divine Mercy, better than the heavens,
Divine Mercy, source of miracles and wonders,
Divine Mercy, encompassing the whole universe,
Divine Mercy, descending to earth in the Person of the
Incarnate Word,
Divine Mercy, which flowed out from the open wound of the
Heart of Jesus,

Divine Mercy, enclosed in the Heart of Jesus for us, and especially for sinners,

Divine Mercy, unfathomed in the institution of the Sacred Host,

Divine Mercy, in the founding of Holy Church,

Divine Mercy, in the Sacrament of Holy Baptism,

Divine Mercy, in our justification through Jesus Christ,

Divine Mercy, accompanying us through our whole life,

Divine Mercy, embracing us especially at the hour of death,

Divine Mercy, endowing us with immortal life,

Divine Mercy, accompanying us at every moment of our life,

Divine Mercy, shielding us from the fire of hell,

Divine Mercy, in the conversion of hardened sinners,

Divine Mercy, astonishment for Angels, incomprehensible to Saints,

Divine Mercy, unfathomed in all the mysteries of God,

Divine Mercy, lifting us out of every misery,

Divine Mercy, source of our happiness and joy,

Divine Mercy, in calling us forth from nothingness to existence,

Divine Mercy, embracing all the works of His hands,

Divine Mercy, crown of all of God's handiwork,

Divine Mercy, in which we are all immersed,

Divine Mercy, sweet relief for anguished hearts,

Divine Mercy, only hope of despairing souls,

Divine Mercy, repose of hearts, peace amidst fear,

Divine Mercy, delight and ecstasy of holy souls,

Divine Mercy, inspiring hope against all hope,

Eternal God, in whom mercy is endless and the treasury of compassion inexhaustible, look kindly upon us and increase Your mercy in us, that in difficult moments we might not despair nor become despondent, but with great confidence submit ourselves to Your holy will, which is Love and Mercy itself.

O incomprehensible and limitless Mercy Divine, To extol and adore You worthily, who can? Supreme attribute of Almighty God, You are the sweet hope for sinful man.

Into one hymn yourselves unite, stars, earth and sea, and in one accord, thankfully and fervently sing of the incomprehensible Divine Mercy.

Chaplet of the Most Precious Blood of Christ

Each bead of the Precious Blood Chaplet is, as it were, a chalice filled with the Divine Blood of Jesus, uplifted by Our Lady to the Eternal Father, imploring every grace necessary for your soul and body. It is prayed on the Rosary of the Precious Blood.

The chaplet consists of seven mysteries in which we meditate on the seven principal bloodsheddings of the Most Precious Blood of Jesus. The beads number thirty-three in honor of the thirty-three years the Precious Blood flowed in the veins of Jesus before it was all poured out on the Cross for our salvation. Its seven petitions unite with each of the seven bloodsheddings, making up seven chapters in the Gospel of Christ's love for me: "He loved me, and delivered Himself up for me."

To pray this chaplet, recite the Our Father on each of the thirty-three beads, completing each of the seven mysteries with the Glory Be and the Concluding Prayer given below, as thanksgiving to the Holy Trinity for this great gift of the Precious Blood. While reciting this chaplet, you are asked to meditate on each of the seven bloodsheddings of Jesus.

O God, come to my assistance! *Lord, make haste to help me!*

Glory be to the Father... *As it was in the beginning...*

1st Mystery
Jesus shed His Blood in the Circumcision.

Let us ask for chastity of soul and body.

Say the Our Father five times and then recite the following: "Incline unto my aid, O God. O Lord, make haste to help me."

Say one Glory Be, and complete the mystery by reciting: "We beseech Thee, therefore, help Thy servants whom Thou has redeemed by Thy Precious Blood."

Our Father (5x)...Glory be to the Father...Final Prayer (said after Glory be to the Father).

2nd Mystery
Jesus shed His Blood whilst praying in the Garden of Olives.

Let us ask for the spirit of prayer.

Say the Our Father five times and then recite the following: "Incline unto my aid, O God. O Lord, make haste to help me."

Say one Glory Be, and complete the mystery by reciting: "We beseech Thee, therefore, help Thy servants whom Thou has redeemed by Thy Precious Blood."

Our Father (5x)...Glory be to the Father...Final Prayer

3rd Mystery
Jesus shed His Blood in the scourging.

Let us ask for the grace of mortification.

Say the Our Father five times and then recite the following: "Incline unto my aid, O God. O Lord, make haste to help me."

Say one Glory Be, and complete the mystery by reciting: "We beseech Thee, therefore, help Thy servants whom Thou has redeemed by Thy Precious Blood."

Our Father (5x)...Glory be to the Father...Final Prayer

4th Mystery
Jesus shed His Blood in the crowning with thorns.

Let us ask for contempt of worldly honors.

Say the Our Father five times and then recite the following: "Incline unto my aid, O God. O Lord, make haste to help me."

Say one Glory Be, and complete the mystery by reciting: "We beseech Thee, therefore, help Thy servants whom Thou has redeemed by Thy Precious Blood."

Our Father (5x)...Glory be to the Father...Final Prayer

5th Mystery
Jesus shed His Blood while carrying His cross.

Let us ask for patience.

Say the Our Father five times and then recite the following: "Incline unto my aid, O God. O Lord, make haste to help me."

Say one Glory Be, and complete the mystery by reciting: "We beseech Thee, therefore, help Thy servants whom Thou has redeemed by Thy Precious Blood."

Our Father (5x)...Glory be to the Father...Final Prayer

6th Mystery
Jesus shed His Blood in the crucifixion.

Let us ask for contrition for our sins.

Say the Our Father five times and then recite the following: "Incline unto my aid, O God. O Lord, make haste to help me."

Say one Glory Be, and complete the mystery by reciting: "We beseech Thee, therefore, help Thy servants whom Thou has redeemed by Thy Precious Blood."

Our Father (5x)...Glory be to the Father...Final Prayer

7th Mystery
Jesus shed His Blood and water when His side was pierced.

Let us ask for the grace of perseverance.

Say the Our Father three times and then recite the following: "Incline unto my aid, O God. O Lord, make haste to help me."

Say one Glory Be, and complete the mystery by reciting: "We beseech Thee, therefore, help Thy servants whom Thou has redeemed by Thy Precious Blood."

Our Father (3x)...Glory be to the Father...Final Prayer

Concluding Prayer

Eternal Father, I offer Thee the most Precious Blood of Jesus Christ in satisfaction for my sins, for the needs of Holy Church and for the relief of the souls in purgatory.

At the end pray the Litany of the Precious Blood.

Litany of the Most Precious Blood of Jesus

Lord, have mercy on us.
Christ, have mercy on us.
Lord, have mercy on us. Christ, hear us.
Christ, graciously hear us.
God the Father of Heaven, *have mercy on us.*
God the Son, Redeemer of the world, *have mercy on us.*
God, the Holy Spirit, *have mercy on us.*
Holy Trinity, One God, *have mercy on us.*
Blood of Christ, only begotten Son of the eternal Father, *save us.*
Blood of Christ, Incarnate Word of God, *etc.*
Blood of Christ, of the New and Eternal Testament,
Blood of Christ, falling upon the earth in the Agony,
Blood of Christ, shed profusely in the Scourging,
Blood of Christ, flowing forth in the Crowning of Thorns,
Blood of Christ, poured out on the Cross,
Blood of Christ, Price of our salvation,
Blood of Christ, without which there is no forgiveness,
Blood of Christ, Eucharistic drink and refreshment of souls,
Blood of Christ, river of mercy,
Blood of Christ, Victor over demons,
Blood of Christ, Courage of martyrs,
Blood of Christ, Strength of confessors,
Blood of Christ, Bringing forth virgins,
Blood of Christ, Help of those in peril,

Blood of Christ, Relief of the burdened,
Blood of Christ, Solace in sorrow,
Blood of Christ, Hope of the penitent,
Blood of Christ, Consolation of the dying,
Blood of Christ, Peace and Tenderness of hearts,
Blood of Christ, Pledge of eternal life,
Blood of Christ, freeing souls from Purgatory,
Blood of Christ, most worthy of all glory and honor,
Lamb of God, who takes away the sins of the world,
Spare us, O Lord.
Lamb of God, who takes away the sins of the world,
Graciously hear us, O Lord.
Lamb of God, who takes away the sins of the world,
Have mercy on us.
You have redeemed us, O Lord, in Your Blood,
And made us, for a God, a kingdom.

Let us pray, Almighty and eternal God, You have appointed Your only-begotten Son the Redeemer of the world and willed to be appeased by His blood. Grant, we beg of You, that we may worthily adore this price of our salvation and through its power be safeguarded from the evils of the present life so that we may rejoice in its fruits forever in heaven. Through the same Christ our Lord. Amen.

The Chaplet of Victory
It is prayed on a regular rosary.
Our Father…Mary…The Apostles' Creed
On the large beads pray:
"They conquered him by the blood of the Lamb and by the word of their testimony." (Rev. 12,11)
On the small beads pray:
Blood of Christ, victor over demons, *save us!*
At the end pray:
Eternal Father, I offer You the most Precious Blood of Jesus Christ in satisfaction for my sins, for the needs of Holy Church and for the relief of the souls in Purgatory.

Praise and thanksgiving be evermore to Jesus who with His Precious Blood has saved us. (3x)

Chaplet of the Holy Wounds

It is prayed on an ordinary rosary.
Sign of the Cross

On the Crucifix: Jesus, Divine Redeemer, be merciful to us and to the whole world. Amen.

First of the three beads: Strong God, holy God, immortal God, have mercy on us and on the whole world. Amen.

Second bead: Grace and mercy, O my Jesus, during present dangers; cover us with Your Precious Blood. Amen.

Third bead: Eternal Father, grant us mercy through the Blood of Jesus Christ, Your only Son; grant us mercy, we beseech You. Amen.

On the large beads: Eternal Father, I offer You the wounds of our Lord Jesus Christ to heal the wounds of our souls.

On the small beads: My Jesus, pardon and mercy through the merits of Your holy wounds.

At the end of the fifth decade recite: Eternal Father, I offer You the wounds of our Lord Jesus Christ, to heal the wounds of our souls. (3x)

Hymn to the Holy Spirit

Come, Holy Ghost, Creator blest,
And in our hearts take up Thy rest;
Come with Thy grace and heav'nly aid,
To fill the hearts which Thou hast made. (2x)

O Comforter, to Thee we cry,
Thou heav'nly gift of God most high,
Thou Fount of life, and Fire of love,
And sweet anointing from above. (2x)

O Finger of the hand divine,
The sevenfold gifts of grace are thine;
True promise of the Father thou,
Who dost the tongue with power endow. (2x)

Thy light to every sense impart,
And shed thy love in every heart;
Thine own unfailing might supply
To strengthen our infirmity. (2x)

Drive far away our ghostly foe,
And thine abiding peace bestow;
If thou be our preventing Guide,
No evil can our steps betide. x2

Praise we the Father and the Son
And Holy Spirit with them One;
And may the Son on us bestow
The gifts that from the Spirit flow. x2

Rosary to the Holy Spirit

It is prayed on a regular rosary.
The Apostles' Creed, Our Father...
On the three small Hail Mary beads after the word Jesus say:
Who through the work of the Holy Spirit may increase our faith!
Who through the work of the Holy Spirit may strengthen our hope!
Who through the work of the Holy Spirit may perfect our love!
Glory be to the Father...
Fatima prayer: Oh my Jesus, forgive us our sins, save us from the fires of hell, and lead all souls to Heaven, especially those in most need of Thy mercy.
On the large beads pray: Our Father...
On the ten small beads pray: Hail Mary...
After the word 'Jesus' say the mysteries of the rosary:
Who may enable our hearts to receive the fullness of grace of the Holy Spirit!
Who may grant us the presence of the Holy Spirit and multiply and strengthen in us three theological virtues!
Who may through the Holy Spirit strengthen us, enlighten, rule over us and guide us on our way to sanctification!
Who may enkindle our hearts with love of the Holy Spirit and fill us with profound humility, loyalty, dedication, strength and holiness!
Who may grant us seven gifts and twelve fruits of the Holy Spirit, may He grant us all the goodness and rebuke from us every evil!
At the end pray:
Holy Spirit, come into my heart and with your power draw me closer to you. Grant me Your love and Your fear. Guard me, Lord Jesus, from every evil thought. Inebriate me with Your love, my Holy Father and my sweet Lord; help me in my every work. Amen!

Litany of the Holy Spirit

Lord, have mercy on us.
Lord, have mercy on us.
Lord, have mercy on us.
God the Father of Heaven, *have mercy on us.*
God the Son, Redeemer of the world, *etc.*
God the Holy Spirit,
Holy Trinity, One God,
Divine Essence, one true God,
Spirit of truth and wisdom,
Spirit of holiness and justice,
Spirit of understanding and counsel,
Spirit of love and joy,
Spirit of peace and patience,
Spirit of longanimity and meekness,
Spirit of benignity and goodness,
Love substantial of the Father and the Son,
Love and life of saintly souls,
Fire ever burning,
Living water to quench the thirst of hearts,
From all evil, *deliver us, O Holy Spirit.*
From all impurity of soul and body, *etc.*
From all gluttony and sensuality,
From all attachments to the things of the earth,
From all hypocrisy and pretense,
From all imperfections and deliberate faults,
From our own will,
From slander,
From deceiving our neighbors,
From our passions and disorderly appetites,
From our inattentiveness to Thy holy inspirations,
From despising little things,
From debauchery and malice,
From love of comfort and luxury,
From wishing to seek or desire anything other than Thee,
From everything that displeases Thee,
Most loving Father, forgive us.

Divine Word, have pity on us.

Holy and divine Spirit, leave us not until we are in possession of the Divine Essence, Heaven of heavens.

Lamb of God, Who takest away the sins of the world,
Send us the divine Consoler.

Lamb of God, Who takest away the sins of the world,
Fill us with the gifts of Thy Spirit.

Lamb of God, Who takest away the sins of the world,
Make the fruits of the Holy Spirit increase within us.

Come, O Holy Spirit, fill the hearts of Thy faithful,
And enkindle in them the fire of Thy love.

Send forth Thy Spirit and they shall be created,
And Thou shalt renew the face of the earth.

Let us pray, God, Who by the light of the Holy Spirit instructed the hearts of the faithful, grant us by the same Spirit to be truly wise and ever to rejoice in His consolation. Through Jesus Christ Our Lord. Amen.

Prayer for the Seven Gifts of the Holy Spirit

Holy Spirit may You grant me:

The gift of the Spirit of Wisdom that I may despise the perishable things of this world and aspire only after the things that are eternal.

The gift of the Spirit of Understanding to enlighten my mind with the light of Your divine truth, the gift of the Spirit of Counsel that I may ever choose the surest way of pleasing God and gaining Heaven.

The gift of the Spirit of Fortitude that I may bear my cross with You, and that I may overcome with courage all the obstacles that oppose my salvation.

The gift of the Spirit of Knowledge that I may know God and know myself and grow perfect in the science of the Saints.

The gift of the Spirit of Piety that I may find the service of God sweet and amiable.

The gift of the Spirit of Fear that I may be filled with a loving reverence towards God, and may dread in any way to displease Him. Mark me, dear Lord, with the sign of Your true disciples and animate me in all things with Your Spirit. Amen.

Holy Spirit, fount of holiness, divine love and truth, we adore You and thank You for all the gifts of grace that You pour on us. Illuminate our reason, make firm our will, clean our hearts, guide our every step and make us ever ready to follow Your inspirations. Forgive us for our lukewarmness in Your service. Do not allow us to ever close our hearts to the call of Your grace. With your aid we are determined to willingly follow all your inspirations so that we may savor the fruits of Your gifts in our souls. Amen.

Our Lady, Star of the Sea (Stella Maris)

Hail, O Star of the ocean,
God's own Mother blest,
ever sinless Virgin,
gate of heav'nly rest.

Taking that sweet Ave,
which from Gabriel came,
peace confirm within us,
changing Eve's name.

Break the sinners' fetters,
make our blindness day,
Chase all evils from us,
for all blessings pray.

Show thyself a Mother,
may the Word divine
born for us thine Infant
hear our prayers through thine.

Virgin all excelling,
mildest of the mild,
free from guilt preserve us
meek and undefiled.

Keep our life all spotless,
make our way secure
till we find in Jesus,
joy for evermore.

Praise to God the Father,
honor to the Son,
in the Holy Spirit,
be the glory one. Amen.

Prayer to Our Lady of Good Health

Here I stand before you, my good Mother, merciful Lady of Good Health. The truth is that due to my sins I am not worthy that you gaze upon me, but still, as your child I completely trust in your motherly care. May you grant my family and me complete health of body and soul. May you convert sinners, so that they never ever offend Jesus and pain you. Help the poor, comfort the inflicted, heal the sick. May you be to all of us our sweet Mother and may we be your good children! Amen.

Prayer to Our Lady of Immediate Assistance

O Mary, Mother of God, you know all the misery and hardships of this world. May you watch ceaselessly over us and over the whole Church of your beloved Son. May you always be Our Lady of Immediate Assistance. Make haste to help us in all our needs. May you be our shelter from this fleeting life and lead us to the everlasting life, through the merits of your Son, Our Lord and Redeemer. Amen.

Litany of the Immaculate Heart of Mary

Lord have mercy upon us.
Christ have mercy upon us.
Christ have mercy upon us. Christ hear us.
Christ graciously hear us.
God the Father of heaven, *have mercy on us.*
God the Son, Redeemer of the world, *have mercy on us.*
God the Holy Ghost, *have mercy on us.*
Holy Trinity, one God, *have mercy on us.*
Heart of Mary, *pray for us.*
Heart of Mary, according to the Heart of God, *etc.*
Heart of Mary, united to the Heart of Jesus,
Heart of Mary, organ of the Holy Ghost,
Heart of Mary, sanctuary of the Divine Trinity,
Heart of Mary, tabernacle of God incarnate,
Heart of Mary, immaculate from thy creation,
Heart of Mary, full of grace,
Heart of Mary, blessed among all hearts,
Heart of Mary, throne of glory,
Heart of Mary, abyss of humility,

Heart of Mary, holocaust of divine love,
Heart of Mary, fastened to the cross with Jesus crucified,
Heart of Mary, comfort of the afflicted,
Heart of Mary, refuge of sinners,
Heart of Mary, hope of the agonizing,
Heart of Mary, seat of mercy,
Lamb of God, who takes away the sins of the world,
Spare us, O Lord.
Lamb of God, who takes away the sins of the world,
Graciously hear, O Lord.
Lamb of God, who takes away the sins of the world,
Have mercy on us.
Christ hear us.
Christ graciously hear us.
Immaculate Mary, meek and humble of heart,
Make our heart according to the Heart of Jesus.

Let us pray. O most merciful God, who, for the salvation of sinners and the refuge of the miserable, was pleased that the Immaculate Heart of the Blessed Virgin Mary should be most like in charity and pity to the Divine Heart of thy Son Jesus Christ; grant that we, who commemorate this most sweet and loving Heart, may, by the merits and intercession of the same blessed Virgin, merit to be found according to the Heart of Jesus. Through the same Christ our Lord. Amen.

Litany of St. Joseph

Lord, have mercy on us.
Christ, have mercy on us.
Lord, have mercy on us. Christ, hear us.
Christ, graciously hear us.
God, the Father of Heaven, *have mercy on us.*
God the Son, Redeemer of the world, *have mercy on us.*
God the Holy Spirit, *have mercy on us.*
Holy Trinity, one God, *have mercy on us.*
Holy Mary, *pray for us.*
St. Joseph, *etc.*
Renowned offspring of David,
Light of Patriarchs,
Spouse of the Mother of God,

Chaste guardian of the Virgin,
Foster father of the Son of God,
Diligent protector of Christ,
Head of the Holy Family,
Joseph most just,
Joseph most chaste,
Joseph most prudent,
Joseph most strong,
Joseph most obedient,
Joseph most faithful,
Mirror of patience,
Lover of poverty,
Model of artisans,
Glory of home life,
Guardian of virgins,
Pillar of families,
Solace of the wretched,
Hope of the sick,
Patron of the dying,
Terror of demons,
Protector of Holy Church,
Lamb of God, who takes away the sins of the world,
Spare us, O Lord!
Lamb of God, who takes away the sins of the world,
Graciously hear us, O Lord!
Lamb of God, who takes away the sins of the world,
Have mercy on us.
He made him the lord of his household.
And prince over all his possessions.

Let us pray. O God, in Your ineffable providence You were pleased to choose Blessed Joseph to be the spouse of Your most holy Mother; grant, we beg You, that we may be worthy to have him for our intercessor in heaven whom on earth we venerate as our Protector: You who live and reign forever and ever. Amen.

Prayer to St. Joseph for the Church

To you, O blessed Joseph, do we come in our tribulation. Through that charity which bound you to the immaculate Virgin Mother of God and through the paternal love with which you embraced the Child Jesus, we humbly beg you to graciously regard the inheritance which Jesus Christ has purchased by His Blood and with your power and strength to aid us in our necessity.

O most watchful Guardian of the Holy Family, defend the chosen children of Jesus Christ. O most loving father, ward off from us every contagion of error and corrupting influence. O our most mighty protector, be propitious to us and from heaven assist us in our struggle with the power of darkness, and as once you rescued the Child Jesus from deadly peril, so now protect God's Holy Church from the snares of the enemy and from all adversity. Shield, too, each one of us by thy constant protection, so that, supported by your example and assistance, we may be able to live piously, to die holy, and to obtain eternal happiness in heaven. Amen.

Prayer to St. Joseph in Tribulations

O blessed father Joseph! Look upon me graciously for I come to you in my needs as your unworthy admirer. I put all my trust in your fatherly aid. I commend to you the salvation of my body and soul. To you I give all the desires of my inner soul and body. I beg you not to let me depart from you without your consolation! I beseech you to teach me through your example how to ever unite my will with God's will, and how to bear my cross with humble patience. I beg you to obtain for me purity of heart, conscience and my body, and all other necessary virtues! I beg you to stand by this poor sinner's side, in my last struggle, so that I may one day, with you and all the chosen children of God, praise Him and love Him in eternity. Amen.

Prayer to St. Joseph for a Happy Death

O Saint Joseph, when the moment arrived of your coming back to the Father's house, Jesus and Mary were standing by your side. Thus, it is just for us Christians to turn to you as the patron and comforter of the dying. We ask you for your assistance in these last moments of our earthly life. Obtain for us the grace to live on this earth just like you did: in righteousness and chastity, in the presence of Jesus and Virgin Mary, never to be parted from them even in our last hour of life. May we, like

you, be accepted in the House of our Father and may our lives be trans-
formed into eternal joy with our Lord. Amen.

Prayer to St. Joseph for the Souls in Purgatory

O blessed Saint Joseph, I humbly beg you to help the poor souls in
Purgatory, so that God Almighty may alleviate their sufferings and
shorten their time. May He make haste and soon grant them to behold
their Creator face to face, whom they ardently long for. I beseech you to
help these poor souls, especially those who are utterly neglected and
seek your assistance, knowing that thy powerful intercession may
obtain all of God's graces. Just like you once assisted Jesus and Mary in
every necessity, so I beg you now to help these poor souls who are
redeemed by the Blood of Jesus Christ and whom our merciful Mother
Mary loves with the most tender affection of her heart. Amen.

Litany of the Saints

Lord, have mercy on us.
Christ, have mercy on us.
Lord, have mercy on us. Christ, hear us.
Christ, graciously hear us.
God, the Father of Heaven, *have mercy on us.*
God, the Son, Redeemer of the world, *have mercy on us.*
God, the Holy Spirit, *have mercy on us.*
Holy Trinity, One God, *have mercy on us.*
Holy Mary, *pray for us.*
Holy Mother of God, *etc.*
Holy Virgin of virgins,
St. Michael,
St. Gabriel,
St. Raphael,
All you holy angels and archangels,
All you holy orders of blessed Spirits,
St. John the Baptist,
St. Joseph,
All you holy patriarchs and prophets,
St. Peter,
St. Paul,
St. Andrew,

St. James,
St. John,
St. Thomas,
St. James,
St. Philip,
St. Bartholomew,
St. Matthew,
St. Simon,
St. Jude,
St. Matthias,
St. Barnabas,
St. Luke,
St. Mark,
All you holy apostles and evangelists,
All you holy disciples of the Lord,
All you holy Innocents,
St. Stephen,
St. Lawrence,
St. Vincent,
Sts. Fabian and Sebastian,
Sts. John and Paul,
Sts. Cosmas and Damian,
Sts. Gervasius and Protasius,
All you holy Martyrs,
St. Sylvester,
St. Gregory,
St. Ambrose,
St. Augustine,
St. Jerome,
St. Martin,
St. Nicholas,
All you holy bishops and confessors,
All you holy doctors,
St. Anthony,
St. Benedict,
St. Bernard,
St. Dominic,
St. Francis,

All you holy priests and levites
All you holy monks and hermits,
St. Mary Magdalen,
St. Agatha,
St. Lucy,
St. Agnes,
St. Cecilia,
St. Catherine,
St. Anastasia,
All you holy virgins and widows,
All you holy men and women, Saints of God
Make intercession for us.
Be merciful,
Spare us, O Lord.
Be merciful,
Graciously hear us, O Lord.
From all evil, *O Lord, deliver us.*
From all deadly sin, *etc.*
From your wrath,
From sudden and unprovided death,
From the snares of the devil,
From anger, and hatred, and all uncleanliness,
From the spirit of fornication,
From lightning and tempest,
From the scourge of earthquake,
From plague, famine and war,
From everlasting death,
Through the mystery of your holy Incarnation,
Through Your Coming,
Through Your Birth,
Through Your Baptism and holy fasting,
Through Your Cross and Passion,
Through Your Death and Burial,
Through Your Resurrection,
Through Your wonderful Ascension,
Through the coming of the Holy Spirit, the Paraclete,
Be merciful to us on the day of judgment,
We sinners, *We beseech you, hear us.*

That You will spare us, *etc.*

That You will pardon us,

That it may please You to bring us to true penance,

Guide and protect our holy Church,

Preserve in holy religion the Pope and all those in holy orders,

Humble the enemies of the Church,

Grant peace and unity to all Christian people,

Bring back to the unity of the Church all who are straying from the truth and bring all unbelievers to the light of the Gospel,

Strengthen and preserve us in Your holy service,

Raise up our minds to desire the things of Heaven,

Render eternal blessings to all our benefactors,

Deliver our souls and the souls of our brethren, relations and benefactors, from eternal damnation,

Give and preserve the fruits of the earth,

Grant eternal rest to all the faithful departed.

The it may please you to hear and heed us,

Jesus, the Living God,

Lamb of God, who takes away the sins of the world,

Spare us, O Lord.

Lamb of God, who takes away the sins of the world,

Graciously hear us, O Lord.

Lamb of God, who takes away the sins of the world,

Have mercy on us.

Christ, hear us.

Christ, graciously hear us.

Lord, have mercy.

Christ, have mercy.

Lord, have mercy on us.

Pray one Our Father.

And lead us not into temptation

But deliver us from evil.

The Chaplet of St. Michael the Archangel

Begin by meditation on the Medal:

O God, come to my assistance.

O Lord, make haste to help me.

Glory be to the Father, to the Son, and to the Holy Spirit.

As it was in the beginning, is now and ever shall be world without end. Amen.

Skip the next four beads, and go to the centerpiece, which will act as the first large, or meditation bead.

Then recite on the first large bead, the centre connector:

Meditation 1. By the intercession of St. Michael and the celestial Choir of Seraphim may the Lord make us worthy to burn with the fire of perfect charity. Amen.

1 Our Father.

On the next three small beads pray:

3 Hail Marys.

On the large bead after the centerpiece connector pray:

Meditation 2. By the intercession of St. Michael and the celestial Choir of Cherubim may the Lord grant us the grace to leave the ways of sin and follow the paths of Christian perfection. Amen.

1 Our Father

3 Hail Marys.

Continue in this way around the circlet of beads, until you reach the last small bead, on which you will pray your last Hail Mary.

Meditation 3. By the intercession of St. Michael and the celestial Choir of Thrones may the Lord infuse into our hearts a true and sincere spirit of humility. Amen.

1 Our Father

3 Hail Marys.

Meditation 4. By the intercession of St. Michael and the celestial Choir of Dominions may the Lord give us grace to govern our senses and overcome any unruly passions. Amen.

1 Our Father

3 Hail Marys.

Meditation 5. By the intercession of St. Michael and the celestial Choir of Powers may the Lord protect our souls against the snares and temptations of the devil. Amen.

1 Our Father

3 Hail Marys.

Meditation 6. By the intercession of St. Michael and the celestial Choir of Virtues may the Lord preserve us from evil and from falling into temptation. Amen.

1 Our Father

3 Hail Marys.

Meditation 7. By the intercession of St. Michael and the celestial Choir of Principalities may God fill our souls with a true spirit of obedience. Amen.

1 Our Father

3 Hail Marys.

Meditation 8. By the intercession of St. Michael and the celestial Choir of Archangels may the Lord grant us perseverance in faith and in all good works in order that we may attain the glory of Heaven. Amen.

1 Our Father

3 Hail Marys.

Meditation 9. By the intercession of St. Michael and the celestial Choir of Angels may the Lord grant us their protection in this mortal life and conducted in the life to come to Heaven. Amen.

1 Our Father

3 Hail Marys.

Upon reaching the end of the circlet, you will come to the centerpiece connector again. Then pray the antiphon:

O glorious prince St. Michael, chief and commander of the heavenly hosts, guardian of souls, vanquisher of rebel spirits, servant in the house of the Divine King and our admirable conductor, you who shine with excellence and superhuman virtue deliver us from all evil, who turn to you with confidence and enable us by your gracious protection to serve God more and more faithfully every day.

On the first pendant bead pray:

1 Our Father.

On the next three beads of the chaplet, pray:

3 Hail Marys.

On the medal of Saint Michael, pray:

Pray for us, most blessed Michael, Prince of the Church of Jesus Christ, *that we may be made worthy of His promises.*

Glory be to the Father and to the Son, and to the Holy Spirit.

As it was in the beginning, is now and ever shall be, world without end. Amen.

Litany of St. Michael the Archangel

Lord, have mercy.
Lord, have mercy.
Christ, have mercy.
Christ, have mercy.
Lord, have mercy.
Lord, have mercy.
God the Father of heaven, *have mercy on us.*
God the Son, Redeemer of the world, *have mercy on us.*
God the Holy Spirit, *have mercy on us.*
Holy Trinity, one God, *have mercy on us.*
St. Michael the Archangel, sword of God, *pray for us.*
St. Michael the Archangel, leader of angels, *etc.*
St. Michael the Archangel, invincible spirit,
St. Michael the Archangel, armed with the strength of God,
St. Michael the Archangel, defender of God,
St. Michael the Archangel, victor over Lucifer,
St. Michael the Archangel, mighty against all demons,
St. Michael the Archangel, mighty against all evil,
St. Michael the Archangel, mighty against witchcraft,
St. Michael the Archangel, intercede for us in our troubles,
St. Michael the Archangel, intercede for us in our ailments,
St. Michael the Archangel, intercede for us in the wars in families and nations,
St. Michael the Archangel, assist us in the combat to defend the Church,
St. Michael the Archangel, assist us in the innermost conflict against temptations,
From the snares of the devil, *deliver us, Lord.*

Let us pray. Almighty and eternal God, who gave us Michael the Archangel as protector and defender, grant that our prayers may deliver us from all evil and the fire of hell. We ask this through Jesus Christ Our Lord. Amen.

Litany of the Guardian Angel

Lord, have mercy on us.

Christ, have mercy on us.

Lord, have mercy on us. Christ, hear us.

Christ, graciously hear us.

God the Father of Heaven. *have mercy on us.*

God the Son, Redeemer of the world. *have mercy on us.*

God the Holy Spirit. *have mercy on us.*

Holy Trinity, One God. *have mercy on us.*

Holy Mary, Queen of Heaven, *pray for us.*

Holy Angel, my guardian, *etc.*

Holy Angel, my protector in all dangers,

Holy Angel, my defense in all afflictions,

Holy Angel, my most faithful lover,

Holy Angel, my preceptor,

Holy Angel, my guide,

Holy Angel, witness of all my actions,

Holy Angel, my helper in all my difficulties,

Holy Angel, my negotiator with God,

Holy Angel, my advocate,

Holy Angel, lover of chastity,

Holy Angel, lover of innocence,

Holy Angel most obedient to God,

Holy Angel, director of my soul,

Holy Angel, model of purity,

Holy Angel, model of docility,

Holy Angel, my counselor in doubt,

Holy Angel, my guardian through life,

Holy Angel, my shield at the hour of death,

Lamb of God, Who takes away the sins of the world,

Spare us, O Lord.

Lamb of God, Who takes away the sins of the world,

Hear us, O Lord.

Lamb of God, Who takes away the sins of the world,

Have mercy on us.

Let us pray. O God, Who with unspeakable providence vouchsafe to send Thy angels to be our guardians, mercifully grant, that we, Thy supplicants, may be always defended by their protection and enjoy their eternal society, through Jesus Christ, Thy Son, Our Lord, Who lives and reigns with You, in the unity of the Holy Spirit, One God, world without end. Amen.

Angel of God, my guardian dear, to whom His love commits me here, ever this day be at my side, to light and guard, to rule and guide. Amen.

Litany of Humility

O Jesus! meek and humble of heart, hear me.
From the desire of being esteemed, *deliver me, my Jesus.*
From the desire of being loved, etc.
From the desire of being extolled,
From the desire of being honored,
From the desire of being praised,
From the desire of being preferred to others,
From the desire of being consulted,
From the desire of being approved,
From the fear of being humiliated,
From the fear of being despised,
From the fear of suffering rebukes,
From the fear of being calumniated,
From the fear of being forgotten,
From the fear of being ridiculed,
From the fear of being wronged,
From the fear of being suspected,
That others may be loved more than I,
Jesus, grant me the grace to desire it.
That others may be esteemed more than I, *etc.*
That, in the opinion of the world, others may increase and I may decrease,
That others may be chosen and I set aside,
That others may be praised and I unnoticed,
That others may be preferred to me in everything,
That others may become holier than I, provided that I may become as holy as I should,

Prayer for Good Priests

Lord, the harvest is abundant and good laborers are few,
so I beseech you:
Enkindle in many young men a holy desire for the priesthood
and a religious vocation!
Grant to all whom You call, the grace never to become weary
and feeble.
Be their light; help them fulfill their divine call!
Give to laborers in your field and garden, firm faith,
unwavering hope and unconditional love! Amen.

Prayer for the Gift of Life

Sweet Lord, You gave me the most priceless gift of life. I greatly rejoice in your gift and I give You thanks and praise for it. I truly desire that my life may be a ceaseless thanksgiving to You. May it be also a help to my brothers and sisters who do not regard this gift with due respect.

I ardently pray for married couples who do not wish to be carriers of life. I also pray for those fathers and mothers who are tempted to forcibly end the life of their unborn child. Enlighten them with Your Holy Spirit so that they may realize the magnitude of fatherhood and motherhood, through which they become Your cooperators in the creation of a new life. Grant them illumination of conscience as to the serious consequences that would result should they refuse to participate in this gift of Yours.

Send forth Your sweet angels to chase away the evil spirit from them and with the intercession of the most Holy Mother of God increase their faith, hope and love. By the merits of the life, suffering and death of Your Son, our Lord Jesus Christ, accept and grant us this petition. Amen. Our Father…

Prayer for the Acceptance of God's Will

My Lord, let Your will be done. Let it be done unto me according to Your will, not mine. I worship You and exalt Your holy will. Let my desires be in accordance with Your desires, let everything be done in the manner that You wish for me. I desire it because it is what You desire for my life and I love You, Lord. Make me more like Jesus, my Redeemer and Savior. Amen.

Act of Abandonment

My God, I trust in Your immense goodness, not just in the goodness that You graciously manifest to the whole world, but in particular the goodness that You show to me, Your poor creature, and how You wisely bestow everything for the greater good of all.

So, my Lord, even when I do not see or understand or feel, I believe that everything that befalls me is an act of Your love. I desire Your will in my present circumstances over any other more pleasing outcome which does not come from You. I surrender myself into Your hands. Mold me in a way that pleases You, and grant that I may find consolation in my abandonment to You. Amen.

Prayer for Married Couples Desiring Children

Mary and Joseph, whom God has granted the grace to know and rejoice in the happiness of parenthood, we beseech you to obtain from our Redeemer the grace of conceiving a healthy child, which we earnestly long for.

However, if it is God's will that we remain childless, we pray that you may encourage us to adopt an abandoned child with love and to raise him for the love of God. Amen.

Prayer of an Expectant Mother for her Child

O Mary, watch over the child that I carry, so that it may always be happy, noble and just.

Help me to love my husband ever more, the father of my child.

I beseech you that my labor may be less painful, even though I am earnestly awaiting the birth of this new creation.

Watch over the doctors who are taking care of me and the baby. Help them to carry out their duties carefully.

O Lord, may the life of this child be for Your greater glory, in health, sickness, success as well as failure.

Lord, You trusted Mary to be the Mother of Your Son. I am grateful that You have entrusted me to be the mother of another child of yours.

Mary, help me to offer all the difficulties of pregnancy and labor with grace and serenity for the good of the child.

Mother Mary, protectress of expectant mothers, pray for us.

Novena Prayer to St. Anthony of Padua

O wonderful St. Anthony, glorious on account of the fame of your miracles, and through the condescension of Jesus coming in the form of a little child to rest in your arms, obtain for me of His bounty the grace which I ardently desire from the depths of my heart. *(State your intention.)*

You who were so compassionate toward miserable sinners, regard not the unworthiness of those who pray to you, but the glory of God that it may once again be magnified, by the granting of the particular request *(State your intention.)* which I now ask for with persevering earnestness. Amen.

Prayer of Liberation from the Spirit of Evil

Jesus, my Savior,
My Lord and my God,
My God and my all,
You who redeemed us by Your sacrifice of the Cross and overthrew the power of Satan,
I beseech You to deliver me from the presence of all evil,
And from every influence of the Evil One.
I beseech You, grant me this favor in Your Name;
I beseech You, grant me this favor by Your Wounds;
I beseech You, grant me this favor by Your Blood;
I beseech You, grant me this favor by Your Cross;
I beseech You, grant me this favor through the intercession of Mary;
Immaculate and sorrowful.
May the Blood and Water that gushed from Your side
Descend upon me and cleanse me,
Deliver me and heal me. Amen.

Prayer Against Every Evil

Spirit of the Lord, Spirit of God, Father, Son and Holy Spirit, Most Blessed Trinity, Immaculate Virgin Mary, Angels, Archangels and all the Saints in heaven, come to my aid.

Purify me, Lord, mould me, fill me, use me.

Drive away from me all evil forces, destroy them, crush them,

That I may feel well and do good.

Drive away from me all spells, witchcraft, black magic, black masses, superstitions, addictions, curses, the evil eye; demonic harassment, demonic possession, obsession; all that is evil and sinful, envy, jealousy, infidelity; physical, mental, moral, spiritual, diabolical, illness.

Destroy all these evils in the fire of hell, that they may never again harm me nor any other creature in the world.

By the strength of Almighty God, in the Name of Jesus Christ, our Savior, though the intercession of the Immaculate Virgin Mary, I order and command all unclean spirits, all the beings that molest me, to depart from me immediately, and forever and to stay in everlasting hell, bound by St. Michael, St. Gabriel and St. Raphael, the Archangels and our guardian angels. May they be crushed under the feet of the most Holy Immaculate Virgin. Amen.

Prayer Against Malefice

Kyrie eleison, God, our Lord, Kings of ages, All-powerful and Almighty, You Who made everything and who transform everything simply by Your will: You Who changed into dew the flames of the 'seven-times hotter furnace' in Babylon and protected and saved the three holy children. You are the doctor and physician of our soul. You are the salvation of those who turn to You. I beseech You to make powerless, banish and drive out every diabolical power, presence and machination; every evil influence, malefic or evil eye and all evil action aimed against me. Where there is envy and malice, give me an abundance of goodness, endurance, victory, and charity.

O Lord, You who love man, I beg You to reach out Your powerful hands and Your most high and mighty arms and come to my aid. Help me, who is made in Your image.

Send Your angel of peace over me, to protect me, body and soul. May he keep at bay and vanquish every evil power, every poison or malice invoked against me by corrupt and envious people. Then under the protection of Your authority may I sing with gratitude: "The Lord is my salvation; whom should I fear? I will not fear evil because You are with me, my God, my strength, my powerful Lord, Lord of peace, Father of all ages."

Lord, our God be merciful to me, Your image, and save your servant from every threat or harm from the evil one, protect me and raise me above all evil; this I beg You through the intercession of our most ever blessed and glorified Lady, Mother of God and ever Virgin Mary, splendid archangels and all Your saints. Amen.

Prayer to the Holy Archangels

Saint Michael the Archangel,
Illuminate us with your light!
O Saint Michael the Archangel,
Shield us beneath your wings!
O Saint Michael the Archangel,
Defend us with your sword!

Saint Raphael the Archangel,
Guard us on our way,
Heal us in our infirmities,
Bring our prayers before the face
Of the God Almighty;
Obtain for us from the Lord
Angelic purity, body and soul.
Saint Gabriel the Archangel,
Help us to truly know
And earnestly fall in love
With the Divine Heart of our Redeemer,
Lord Jesus Christ, and with the Immaculate Heart
Of His and our most holy and kind Mother Mary,
The Queen of heaven and earth!

Private Exorcism

Anyone can apply this form of prayer for himself, as well as for others who are not present during the prayer. First, one should make the Sign of the Cross using holy water and then say out loud the given prayer, if possible. It is especially helpful in difficult situations, temptations and trials, in time of great fear and confusion, of anxiety attacks and trepidation, when one is in despair, before starting important business or making decisions, when one is confronted with hostile and antagonistic individuals, and primarily in sickness and at the hour of death.

IN THE NAME OF JESUS AND MARY,
I command you, infernal evil spirits, to be banished from us (him, her, them), from this place (his, her, their), and never dare to come back to seek us and harm us in any way!
Jesus, Mary (3x).

Saint Michael the Archangel, fight for us!

Our holy guardian angels protect us (him, her, them) from all the snares of the evil adversary!

And may the blessing of the Father, the love of the Son, and the power of the Holy Spirit, the motherly protection of our Heavenly Queen, assistance of our guardian angel and intercession of all the saints always be with us (him, her, them), everywhere and for all ages. Amen!

Prayer for Physical Healing

Lord Jesus, through that faith which You gave to me at Baptism, I worship You and thank You.

You are the Son of God who became man. You are the Messiah, the Savior.

At this moment I want to say to You like Peter did: there is no other name under heaven given to men by which we are to be saved.

I accept You, Lord Jesus, in my heart and in my life;

I want You to take absolute lordship over my life.

Forgive me my sins just like You forgave the sins of the paralytic in the Gospel.

Cleanse me with Your divine Blood!

I lay down at Your feet all my sufferings and infirmities. Heal me, Lord, by the power of Your glorified Wounds, by the power of Your Cross and Your Most Precious Blood! You are the Good Shepherd and I am but one of the sheep from Your flock: take pity on me!

Jesus, You are the One who said: ask and it will be given to you.

The people from Galilee brought their sick before You and You healed them. You never change. Your power is the same. I believe that You can heal me for You have the same compassion for me that You felt towards the sick whom You encountered because You are the Resurrection and Life.

Thank You, Jesus, for what You will do for me.

I accept the plan of Your Love for me. I believe that You will reveal Your glory to me.

Before even knowing how You will come to my aid, I praise You and thank You.

Amen.

Prayer for Inner Healing

Lord Jesus, You came to heal our wounded and troubled hearts. I beg You to heal the torments that cause anxiety in my heart; I beg You, in a particular way, to heal all that is the cause of sin. I beg You to come into my life and heal me from my emotional traumas that came upon me in my early years and from the wounds caused by these traumas throughout my whole life! Lord Jesus, You know all my burdens. I lay them on Your Good Shepherd's Heart. I beseech You, by the merits of the great, open wound in Your heart, to heal the small wounds that are in me. Heal the pain of my memories, so that nothing that has happened to me will cause me to remain in pain and anguish, filled with anxiety.

Heal, O Lord, all those wounds that have been the cause of all the sins that are rooted in my life. I want to forgive all those who have offended me. Tend to those inner sores that make me unable to forgive. You, who came to heal afflicted hearts, please heal my own heart.

Heal, my Lord Jesus, those intimate wounds that are the cause of my physical illness. I offer You my heart. Accept it, Lord, purify it and give me the sentiments of Your Divine Heart. Help me to be meek and humble.

Heal me, O Lord, from the pain caused by the death of my loved ones, which is oppressing me. Grant that I may regain peace and joy in the knowledge that You are the Resurrection and the Life. Make me an authentic witness to Your Resurrection, Your victory over sin and death and Your living presence among us! Amen.

Prayer of Surrender

O Lord, cleanse me from everything that is not Yours. I want to be a pure vessel of Yours and I offer myself unconditionally to You. I want to be thoroughly Yours; cleanse me from every obstacle that prevents me from serving You without fear. Implant in me, Lord, the seed of Your love so that I may love everyone and burn with love for others. Lord, save me from myself, from my selfish 'I' that is always rebellious, so that I may peacefully navigate with You the ocean of Your love. I want Your love to transform me into You, so that I may not live anymore, but You, Christ, live in me. I surrender my heart, soul, body, mind, my memories and my will to You; I put them at Your disposal, into Your hands and Your holy will. Do with me whatever pleases You, guide me, strengthen me, restore me and invigorate me. I surrender and entrust to You my family and my everything. I consecrate myself to

152

Your Precious Heart and to the Immaculate Heart of Your kind Mother. I want to renew this prayer of surrender every day and thus remain aware of Your love and mercy. Lord, You are my safeguard, my mercy and love that cover all of my faults. Amen.

Prayer for Sanctification and Renewal

Lord, grant me a pure and obedient heart, a simple and humble heart, dedicated and honest. I want to be honest, simple, humble and full of love for others, but I fail. Lord, break down all the barriers, rend all the bonds inside me so that I may fight them with Your Mercy. I want to love, I want to be healed, I want to become a better person, changed and more like You!

Come, Lord Jesus; come, Lord, and tear down all the barriers and all the bondages in me. Deliver me from every evil of the body and soul, heal me! I renounce every evil doing and I firmly believe that You will free me and cure me. Let Your holy will be done unto me. Grant me the grace to fight! I want to love, I want to be healed, I want to become a better person and changed more unto Your image.

Come, Lord Jesus, and with Your almighty power and Your love crush down all the walls, all that prevents me from coming to You. Jesus, seal with Your Blood every evil that threatens me, heal my wounds, cleanse all the destruction and debris inside me, I want to be holy! I want to cooperate with You; I want Your Holy Spirit to lead me into the whole truth. May You grow in me Lord. My 'self' is big, I want it to disappear. I want to be little, simple, I want to become holy.

Help me, Lord, to obtain with Your mercy all that I desire. Grant me the grace, Lord, to fight; to always be aware of Your love, patience, mercy and forgiveness. Give me the grace of true repentance, that in every moment I confess to myself and to You, God, that I repent with a contrite heart every time for offending and wounding Your Heart. Repentance, repentance, grant me contrite repentance so that I do not abuse Your mercy anymore.

Without Your mercy, Lord, I cannot do anything right, nor can you, Lord, pour Your grace on me, if I don't open up myself to You, if I don't cooperate with You. Open my heart Lord, always be in my thoughts, my words and my deeds. Strengthen me, cleanse me, deliver me, enable me, renew me, heal me, heal my soul, heal my body, purify my thoughts, wash me with Your Blood! I am poor, I am weak, miserable and inconstant. I say one thing and do another. Spirit demands what is of spirit and flesh demands what is of flesh: I fight back poorly,

I despair. When things go wrong I do not accept myself. Grant me the grace of accepting myself and others! Grant me the grace to forgive myself and others! Lord, embrace my heart with Your Spirit! Enlighten my reason; strengthen my will to accept Your will. Pour Your holy Spirit on me! Bring me peace and love, firm faith, alive and adamant hope!

Come, Holy Spirit; come, Holy Spirit and restore my spirit so that I may fulfill the will of the Father through You and with You! Come, Holy Spirit; come, Lord Jesus and burn up with Your love everything that is in me! Come, Lord Jesus; come, Lord Jesus and let the fire of Your love burn everything that is in me, come Lord Jesus, come Lord Jesus, come Lord Jesus, do not be late! May Your precious Blood boil, circulate through my veins, through my heart and thoughts! Everything that is in me, Lord, You renew and sanctify! You called us to be holy. Thank You for wanting to sanctify us all.

Be blessed, Jesus, in the Most Blessed Sacrament! Be blessed, Jesus, in every soul! Change, Jesus, all of us, our families; deliver, renew us all; heal us, Lord, in our bodies and souls!

Jesus, liberate me from every fear, consideration, pride, self-love, anxiety, anger, unforgiveness, from every evil of body and soul! Jesus, Jesus, Jesus, open up my heart, open up my heart! Open, Lord, and call all hearts to come back to you! Jesus, Jesus, Jesus I want to live only in Your presence; I want to cooperate with You and unite myself to You forever!

Jesus, Jesus, Jesus thank You for everything that You gave me, that You are giving me right now and what You will give me! Thank You for Your Holy Spirit who is teaching us how to pray! Thank You for sending us Your Spirit to teach us, guard us, defend us, enlighten us, sanctify us and lead us to Your Father!

Come, Jesus! Come, Jesus! Come, Holy Spirit! Come, Holy Spirit, into every heart and soul! Come, Lord Jesus!

Maranatha! Maranatha! Maranatha! Amen! Alleluia!

Prayer for Inner Healing

Jesus, by Your love, goodness and mercy, I beseech You to enter into the root cause of my present state. I beg You to enter into the roots of all my traumas, fears, shock that I have experienced in my mother's womb, in my childhood and in my life. Come, Lord Jesus, in that wounded area. Drench me with Your Precious Blood; cleanse me, deliver me, heal me. Come, Lord Jesus, fill my heart with love and faith so that I may believe You, Jesus, that you were present in all those moments of wounding and all those situations. Grant me the grace to be able to feel Your embrace, warmth, and holy presence. Soothe my entire being that was in turmoil, scared, wounded and inflicted.

Christ, my God, bring PEACE into my heart. May Your PEACE take over my whole being, the peace that only You can give.

Christ, my God, heal me, heal in me that area of my wounded childhood. Free me from the pain that was caused then; from fear, shock, anxiety, hatred that was poured down on me. Banish all that back then deeply wounded my heart and negatively burdened my mind. You, Jesus, can do everything. You were present then, let me believe You, that in those moments You were present there, when I was afflicted by and angry at those who hurt me. Banish, Lord, all the wrath, unforgiveness, rejection, sorrow which filled my heart then. Jesus bring into that place love, peace and joy of Your presence. Fill me with the Holy Spirit. Heal me from unforgiveness and 'unacceptance.' Fill me with forgiving and healing power. Let Your love infuse my heart and penetrate every corner of my heart so that I may always, with a prepared heart, love others and forgive, give myself and be at Your disposal Lord, the way You want me to be.

Thank You, Jesus! Thank You, Jesus! Thank You, Jesus!

I praise You, Jesus! I glorify you, Jesus! I honor Your Name!

Jesus, I love You!

I surrender myself to You! Do with me what You desire. I surrender myself to You through Mary, guide me through her. Amen.

Anima Christi

Soul of Christ, sanctify me; Body of Christ, save me; Blood of Christ, inebriate me; Water from the side of Christ, wash me; Passion of Christ, strengthen me; O good Jesus, hear me; within Your wounds, hide me; let me never be separated from You; from the Evil One, protect me; at the hour of my death, call me; and bid me come to You; that with Your saints, I may praise You forever and ever. Amen.

Magnificat

My soul magnifies the Lord,
And my spirit rejoices in God my Savior.
For He has regarded the low estate of His handmaiden,
For behold, henceforth all generations shall call me blessed.
For He who is mighty has done great things for me, and holy

is His name.

And His mercy is on those who fear Him from generation to generation.

He has shown strength with His arm:

He has scattered the proud in the imagination of their hearts.

He has put down the mighty from their thrones,

and exalted those of low degree.

He has filled the hungry with good things;

and the rich He has sent empty away.

He has helped His servant Israel, in remembrance of His mercy;

As He spoke to our fathers, to Abraham and to his posterity forever.

Glory be to the Father and to the Son and to the Holy Spirit.

As it was in the beginning, is now and ever shall be, world without end. Amen.

Personal Consecration to the Sacred Heart of Jesus

O most Sacred Heart of Jesus, the source of every goodness, I adore You, I believe in You, I trust in You, I love You and I am sorry for all my sins. I give to You this poor heart of mine. Make it humble, patient, pure so that it may comply with all Your desires.

Let me, O good Jesus, live in You and You in me. Protect me in dangers, comfort me in hardships and pains, and grant me health of soul and body, bless all my work and grant me the grace of a holy death. Amen.

Personal Consecration to the Immaculate Heart of Mary

O most Holy Virgin Mary, my Mother and my Queen, I consecrate and give to your Immaculate Heart my whole being: my thoughts, words and work; my spirit, soul and body. Dispense with my entire being and with everything that I own, now and in eternity, for the praise and glory of the Holy Trinity, for the consecration of the Church and the salvation of the world.

My Immaculate Mother, help me to live a life worthy of my baptismal sanctification so that I may belong irrevocably to my Redeemer. Let me be like you, willing to hear the promptings of the Holy Spirit! May God's will be fulfilled in me and through me always. Amen.

Examination of Conscience

Preparation for a good confession

First of all we should be asking ourselves the following questions:

When was my last confession?

Was my last confession valid?

Did I perform the penance I was given in my last confession?

Did I make up for the evil that I did to my neighbor?

How often do I go to confession?

Have I been living for a long period of time in the state of grave sin causing me to feel weighed down and lifeless?

(To live a deep spiritual life, frequent confession is advised, for example, once a month, and to receive Holy Communion every Sunday, as well as on important feast days).

Do I approach the Sacrament of Penance with a sincere intention to clean my soul and relieve it from the burden of sin, to renew my life and to turn to and deepen my friendship with God, or do I perhaps partake this sacrament out of habit, without real zeal to repair my life?

Do I truly repent of my sins? Do they cause me sorrow and remorse because they are ruining my life?

Do I sincerely renounce every sin? Have I sincerely resolved not to sin any more or do I plan to commit the same sins again?

(If there is no true contrition in the penitent and a firm desire to stop sinning with deliberate concealment of a grave sin, then the sacrament is not valid and the sins are not forgiven. Thus we just add on a new sin, that is, we blasphemously confess our sins without an earnest intention of receiving the holy sacrament of Christ in contrition. Every confession is an act of conversion and renouncement of every — even the smallest — sin and a complete adherence to Christ and to life in His love and mercy.)

"How many have perished for faulty confession?" — This is one of the famous quotes from St. Teresa of Avila.

Sins Against the Ten Commandments

1. I AM THE LORD YOUR GOD! YOU SHALL HAVE NO OTHER GODS BEFORE ME!

Does God have the first place in my life? ("My God, my all," as St. Frances of Assisi would say).

Do I have any other gods besides Him (money and material goods, career, fortune, respect, power, desire to be liked by others, absorbed with fashion and physical appearance, preoccupation with body and flesh, social prestige among family and friends, self-love, etc.)?

Do I have other idols or gods like sport celebrities, rock stars, politicians and actors, or perhaps things like my electronic devices (computers, smart phones, tablets, video games, tv, etc.), cars, houses, or other items?

Do I have any doubts concerning the faith? Do I dedicate enough of my time to God?

Do I pray regularly or do I skip my prayers on occasion or for a long period of time? Do I have a superficial approach to faith?

Do I put enough effort into reading about God (the Bible, religious material and books) and working on strengthening my faith, or am I lazy and indifferent?

Do I earnestly search for God — real Truth and true Joy — with an open heart?

Do I truly believe that God will help me in my life? Am I superstitious? Do I practise or follow superstitions such as: black cat or the number 13, astrology, palm reading or any occult or similar practice?

Do I knock on wood three times in order for the good things in my life not to get ruined? Do I visit psychic healers, therapeutic touch healers, self-named prophets, dowsers and others? (Many chiropractors are involved with energy healing; some kinds of acupuncture treatments are of magical origin...).

Did I take courses in transcendental meditation or yoga, or did I participate in any rituals of oriental sects, like Hare Krishna, Vipassana Buddhist (mindfulness meditation)?

Was I involved in Sai Baba's movement, Baha'i movement or other oriental or Eastern religious movements?

Was I a member of some sect or secret society (Masons)? Did I perform any divination myself (divination from coffee grounds, palm reading or tarot card reading)? Did anybody else perform something for or on me? Do I read horoscopes, or do I believe in astrology?

Do I love God, praise Him and glorify Him?

Was I thankful to God for all the good things in my life, thus becoming more open to receiving greater gifts?

Was I silent about my faith for my benefit, profit, consideration, or due to embarrassment or fear? Did I keep company with people who derided the Faith or religious truths, or with anyone who showed an anti-religious attitude?

Have I been a member of some socially liberal party that relativizes moral issues, or of a (communist) party that denies God? To whom and to what do I give first place in my life? Who is my god?

2. YOU SHALL NOT TAKE THE NAME OF THE LORD YOUR GOD IN VAIN!

This includes swearing, the breaking of vows, taking the name of God and/or the saints in vain, showing a lack of respect for the sanctity of God's name, using profane language, cursing and frequent and unnecessary mentioning of Satan's name.

3. REMEMBER TO KEEP HOLY THE SABBATH DAY!

Failing to attend Mass on Sundays and/or official Feast Days is a grave sin.

Working on Sundays or on official Feast Days. Doing regular everyday chores on Sundays. (The Lord's Day must be different from other days of the week, and has to be more dedicated to God.)

Studying on Sundays and on official Feast Days without some great need. Being late for Mass and conversing during Mass. Being distracted at Mass. Attending Mass out of habit. Not believing in the validity, greatness and spiritual benefit of the Holy Mass. Shunning of the religious devotions, like Stations of the Cross and similar devotions…

Minimalism in faith. (That is, doing the bare minimum required by the norms of the Church and nothing more.)

Not giving any charity or alms for the purposes of the Church or the poor. Eating meat on Fridays and not observing the fast on Ash Wednesday, Good Friday or any other days mandated by the Church.

4. HONOR YOUR FATHER AND YOUR MOTHER..

This includes showing disrespect or disobedience to parents, elders, teachers and superiors. Disrespect for parental authority. Neglecting parents and showing ingratitude towards them. Parents shouldn't make children's life bitter or hinder God's will for their lives. They should ask themselves whether they give a good example of Christian love and virtue to their children. Do they take care of their children's physical, material and spiritual needs? Do they teach their children how to pray? Do they impart religious truths and Christian morals? Do they pay attention to what their children do, whom they associate with and where they hang out? Do they monitor their activities to ensure that the content entering their minds is of sound Christian morals?

5. YOU SHALL NOT KILL!

Murder. Abortion. Suicide. Fights. Conflicts. Quarrels. Offenses. Immoderate consumption of food and beverages. Giving bad examples. Drugs. Excessive smoking and drinking. Damaging the health of oneself and others. Menacing and torturing others. Humiliating and accusing others. Wishing evil or death to oneself or others. Revenge. Hatred. Unforgiveness. Grumpiness. Pessimism. Self-pity. Participating or persuading another to have an abortion (the severity of guilt is equal for both a father and a mother) or to commit murder. Infanticide. Anger, wrath, fury. Pride. Envy. Egoism. Avarice. Excessive self-centricity. Excessive selectiveness and gourmet disposition in food. Damaging one's health with excessive dieting for the sake of outer appearance.

Showing disrespect for God's natural laws, for example for the natural cycle of days and nights. (For example, going late to bed and oversleeping until after 10 a.m.) Hanging out in gloomy, dark, smoky and noisy disco clubs or bars; staying up late until early morning. Lewd parties of any kind. Dancing in close, intimate, contact with others or erotic disco dancing. Excessive time spent in pubs and neglecting family responsibilities. Gambling for money of any kind. Avoiding any type of ascetic discipline. Laziness and erratic behavior of any kind. Excessive watching of TV programs. Failing to study/work adequately or meet school/work obligations. Ignoring one's family or one's family obligations.

6. YOU SHALL NOT COMMIT ADULTERY!

Impure lustful thoughts, words and deeds. Lascivious gaze. Reading and watching pornographic and shameful films, books and magazines.

Engaging in French kissing (so-called movie kisses), petting, indecent and immoral behavior, sexual intercourse — before marriage.

Adultery. Masturbation. Homosexual relations. Using any type of artificial contraception including abortifacients (morning after pill), mechanical devices like coils and diaphragms and condoms which prevent conception. Interruption of intercourse in marriage (marital onany — Gen. 38, 9). For planning a family, the method of natural family planning (NFP) using fertile and non-fertile days is allowed, which is the most recommended for edifying marital love.

Sterilization and artificial insemination are also grave sins.

Excessive sensuality and obsession with sex and with the opposite sex, perverse marital acts, avoiding and being fearful of having children, prideful attitude in either husband or wife.

Living in an unsacramental (common law) marriage is also a great sin. Frequenting nudist beaches.

Indecent or provocative dress, like too tight, too short or too revealing clothing; everything that accentuates the body figure too much.

7. YOU SHALL NOT STEAL!

Stealing. Stealing things from businesses, individuals or public places.

Destroying public property and social assets.

Fraud of any kind. Money earned through corrupt and dishonest practices and the exploitation of others (unjust profit, shady business practices), damaging others, not paying one's debts (We are to return whatever amount has been stolen, or we are to give to the poor the closest equivalent amount of money.) Avarice, greed for money and material goods. Envy. Receiving bribes. Showing diminished respect for the work and efforts of others. Freeloading train and bus rides, if we have the money to buy a ticket. Insufficient effort and irresponsibility in work.

8. YOU SHALL NOT BEAR FALSE WITNESS AGAINST YOUR NEIGHBOR!

Small and big lies. Dishonesty. Bragging. Unnecessary and excessive talking. Derogatory conversation. Dirty jokes. Frivolity. Calumny. False promises. Vanity. Gossiping. Criticizing. Objecting. Accusing and judging others. Damaging the good reputation of others. Irresponsibility. Indifference. Lacking compassion for the suffering of others.

9. YOU SHALL NOT COVET YOUR NEIGHBOR'S WIFE!

Desiring your neighbor's spouse, committing adultery with him or her. Being too intimate and seeing too often a neighbor's spouse. Failing to avoid such sinful occasions. Scandalizing any member of one's own or a neighbor's family, especially the children. Participating in any way in offending the sanctity of marriage. Causing discord in a marriage or a marriage breakup.

10. YOU SHALL NOT COVET YOUR NEIGHBOR'S GOODS!

Envying others or being jealous about their possessions or trying to compete materially with them. Being obsessed with making or spending money and the accumulation of wealth and material goods. Spiritual envy. Slander against the good reputation of others out of malice, jealousy or imprudence.

Neglecting the spiritual dimension of man, which man in fact lives on.

Jesus says that one does not live by bread alone, but by every word that comes forth from the mouth of God and that we should seek first the Kingdom of God and His righteousness, and all other things will be given us besides.

Letters of Support

NUNTIATURA APOSTOLICA IN CROATIA

Zagreb, March, 2nd 2000

The Reverend Monsignor,

I have received Your book "How to recognize the snares of the Evil One," for which I am most sincerely grateful. I truly think that it is necessary to pay special attention to the topics which Your book is dealing with.

With the expressions of deep respect and remaining devoted to God.

+ Gulio Einaudi, the Apostolic Nuncio.

Hvar, March, 7th 2000.

Dear Monsignor,

I greatly THANK You for the wonderful GIFT — "How to recognize the snares of the Evil One." I wish you further success with this kind of astute work.

Regards and blessing in Christ

+ Slobodan Stambuk,

Bishop of Hvar — Brac and Vis diocese.

The Reverend Monsignor,

Gospic, March, 7th 2000.

I have received Your beautifully equipped and even more beautifully written book, for which I am very thankful. It is a manual about the Evil One and a prayer book against him. I believe that many people will find numerous instructions and motivation on how to fight against the Evil inside them as well as in the outside world.

With respect and regards,

Mosignor Mile Bogovic,

Auxiliary Bishop

THE DIOCESE OF POZEGA

Pozega, March, 2nd, 2000.

Office of the Bishop of Pozega,

The Most Reverend Sir!

We have received your book "How to recognize the snares of the Evil One," which you sent to the most Venerable Bishop as a sign of your honest respect. He thanks you for your valuable gift that is going to grab the attention of many readers with its content and enrich our bishopric library fund.

With sincere regards in our Lord,

Perica Matanovic,

Head of the Office.

Porec, March, 6th 2000

The Most Reverend Monsignor,

I thank You for the book that You have sent me; I congratulate you on the effort that you have put into it! I have briefly taken a look at it and I find it very interesting and real! May God make it a means of help for many.

With sincere regards,

+ Ivan Milovan, Bishop of Porec — Pula diocese.

164

Krk, April, 19th 2000

I hereby confirm that I have received the gift of the copy of your book "How to recognize the snares of the Evil One."

From the bottom of my heart I thank you for the gift.

May the celebration of the Resurrection in this year of the Great Jubilee grant you the firmness of your faith in order for all the graves and ruins of the human events to be risen victoriously in the image of Christ, the Ruler Almighty, to whom all the times and centuries belong. May He, who lives everlastingly among us in the Eucharist, be the stronghold of your hope and sustain you in your living hardships.

Invoking over your work the abundance of God's blessings, I send you sincere regards in Our Lord!

+ Valter Zupan,

Bishop of Krk diocese

The Most Honorable Father, General Vicar,

I have received your book "How to recognize the snares of the Evil One." As soon as I received the book I browsed through it and became your supporter. I congratulate you for your bold faith! In particular I am surprised that you, General Vicar, are also the author of this book. I congratulate the father Bishop Ivan for his courage to choose such a General Vicar in his service, specifically in times when the Church is becoming more and more secularized. May we not be afraid of the devil, the cunning Evil One.

With special regards,

Yours in Christ and in our Dear Lady,

Monsignor Frane Franic, Archbishop emeritus of Split-Makarska

About the Author

Monsignor Milivoj Bolobanić was born on 15th February 1937 on the Croatian island of Olib, near Zadar. He finished the four-year elementary school in 1947 and the eight-year classical grammar school at the Archbishopric Seminary Zmajević in Zadar in 1954. He graduated in theology in 1962 from the Catholic Seminary in Zagreb and was ordained a priest on 29th June 1961. He served as parish priest in Privlaka, Zemunik and at the Shrine Church of St. Simon (sveti Šime) in Zadar, also covering the parish of Crno.

During the Homeland War he was parish priest and dean in Biograd na moru. He also served as dean in the deaconries of Zemunik and Zadar. In his two last terms he was elected secretary of the Council of Priests of the Zadar Archbishopric, and he also held the office of president of the Diocesan Council for the celebration of the Great Jubilee of Christianity in 2000. He held the responsible office of general vicar of the Zadar Archbishopric. He was parish priest there at the Cathedral of St. Anastasia (sveta Stošija). Since 2006 he has been the parish priest at the parish of St. Mary, Queen of Peace in Zadar.

Apart from his well-developed parish pastoral work, which clearly demonstrates the parish as the fellowship of fellowships, he endeavours on a daily basis to help people who are in some way under the influence of the Evil One. From time to time he helps his fellow priests in their pastoral work, leading spiritual renewals in Croatia and abroad. His many seminars on deliverance and healing have borne much fruit in those who have the desire to make fundamental changes in their lives and live in obedience to God's commandments.

Monsignor Milivoj Bolobanić's very popular book "How to Recognize and Protect Oneself Against the Snares of the Evil One" (Kako prepoznati zamke Zloga) has gone into its seventh, extended edition, in Croatian. Its Foreword was written by the well-known president of the International Association of Exorcists Don Gabriele Amorth. The book has been published in Italian, English and German.

He spends a large amount of time every day visiting people seeking spiritual assistance – in deep conversation, holy confession, spiritual counselling and prayer for deliverance and healing of their body and soul. He prays for exorcism for individual cases when he believes it to be necessary, with the approval of his bishop.

Every first Sunday in the month he has a special prayer program in his parish church which is attended by people from various parts of Croatia and the neighbouring countries – Slovenia and Bosnia and Herzegovina. The program begins at 4 p.m. with the rosary and confession, where he is helped by several other priests. Holy Mass is then celebrated, after which the Blessed Sacrament is exhibited and prayers for deliverance and healing of soul and body are said before it. The adoration ends with a blessing and Benediction. At the end of the prayer program any one who wants and who feels the need may come forward for laying on of hands and personal, individual prayer. An increasing number of young people who feel a desire for God and who are seeking an answer to their spiritual problems and deliverance from the effects of dabbling in the occult come to this prayer program.

Every year he holds 10 to 15 spiritual renewals in Croatia, lasting between 3 and 7 days, and sometimes he also holds spiritual renewals in European countries, and in the USA, Canada and Australia.

Translation: Ivana Pesic, Jim Singer

Reviewers: Wendy Cassibault, Ksenia Choly, Rosemary Getty, Janice Glover, Claudine Goller, Maureen Kinlin, Jaroslawa Kisyk.

Bibliography

Amorth G., Egzorcist govori, Jelsa, 1995.
An Exorcist Speaks

Amorth G., Egzorcisti i psihijatri, Jelsa, 2005.
Exorcists and Psychiatrists

Amorth G., Izvjesca rimskog egzorcista, Djakovo, 2002.
An Exorcist Tells His Story

Amorth G., Novi izvjestaji jednog egzorcista, Jelsa, 1997.
An Exorcist: More Stories

Atti, del Corso., Esorcismo e preghiera di liberazione, Editrice Shalom, 2005.

Autexier, E., Tajna zla, Djakovo, 1995.
The Mystery of Evil

Bamonte F., Possessioni diaboliche ad esorcismo, Milano, 2006.

Bamonte F., I danni dello spiritismo, Roma, 2003.

Bartz W., Sekte danas, Zagreb, 1984.
Today's Sects

Baumer U., Hocemo samo tvoju dusu, Zagreb, 1998.
We just Want Your Souls

Betancourt D., Ozdravljeni duhom, Zagreb, 1998.
Healed by the Spirit

Betancourt D. Ustani i hodi, Jelsa, 1994.
Get Up and Walk

Blazevic J. Proroci novog doba, Zagreb, 2001.
Prophets of the New Age

Bobas A., Rock-glazba i sotonizam, Zagreb, 1998.
Rock music and Satanism

Bubalo R., Pogled u krajeve srca, Zagreb, 1999.
Glance Into the Depths of Hearts

Chenesseau R., Diario di un prete esorcista.
Convegno internazionale degli esorcisti, Collevalenza, 2002.

De Grandis R., Obnovljeni Duhom Svetim, Zagreb, 2001.
Renewed by the Spirit

De Grandis R., Pocivanje u duhu, Zagreb, 2001.
Resting in the Spirit

De Grandis R., Rastimo u Gospodinu, Zagreb, 2001.
Growing in Jesus

De Grandis R, Rijec spoznanja, Zagreb, 2001.
Word of Knowledge

De Grandis R., Sluzba ozdravljanja, Zagreb, 2001.
Forgiveness is Healing

De Grandis, R. Svjedocanstvo mog zivota, Zagreb, 2001.
Testimony of Fr. R. DeGrandis, SSJ

Dokumenti Drugog vatikanskog koncila, Zagreb, 1970.
Documents of the Second Vatican Council

Ernetti P. Kateheza Sotone, Jelsa, 2004.
Catechesis of Satan

Faricy P. Molitva i nutarnje ozdravljenje, Jelsa, 1998.
Prayer for Inner Healing

Fusco P. Preghiere di liberazione dal maligno, Firenca, 2001.

Glavurtic M ., Pakao, Sion, 1998.
Hell

Glavurtic M. Satana, Beograd, 1978.
Satan

Godfried D., Krist ili vodenjak?, Split, 1998.
Christ or Aquarius?

Gutierrez G. Teologija oslobodjenja, Zagreb, 1989.
The Liberation Theology

Huber G. Odlazi sotono, Djakoovo, 1993.
Go Away Satan

Ivancic T., A vi ovako molite, Zagreb, 1992.
And You, Pray This Way

Ivancic T., Agresivnost i povjerenje, Zagreb, 2000.
Aggressiveness and Trusting

Ivancic T. Ako oprostis, Zagreb, 1997.
If You Forgive

Ivancic T. Dijagnoza duse i hagioterapija, Zagreb, 2004.
Diagnosis of the Soul and Hagiotherapy

Ivancic T. Kako duhovno pomoci covjeku?, Zagreb, 1996.
How to Help Man Spiritually

Ivancic T. Hagioterapija i pastoral Crkve, Zagreb, 1996
Hagiotherapy and Pastoral Work of the Church

Ivancic T. Lijeciti brak i obitelj, Zagreb, 1995.
Healing of Marriage and Family

Ivancic T. Molitva koja lijeci, Zagreb, 1994.
Prayer That Heals

Ivancic T. Otkrice duhovne terapije, Zagreb, 1998.
Discovery of Spiritual Therapy

Ivancic T., Ovisnost i sloboda, Zagreb, 2000.
Dependence and Liberty

Ivancic T., Reinkarnacija i uskrsnuce, Zagreb, 1999.
Reincarnation and Resurrection

Ivancic T., Susret sa zivim Bogom, Zagreb, 1985.
Encounter With The Living God

Ivancic T., Za umorne, Zagreb, 1985.
For the Weary

Katekizam Katolicke Crkve, Zagreb, 1994.
Catechism of the Catholic Church

Kongregacija za naukl vjere: Naputak o molitvama kojima se od Boga moli ozdravljenje, Zagreb, 2001.
Instructions on Prayers for Healing

Letic F., Protokoli sionskih mudraca, Zagreb, 1996.
Protocols of the Wise Men of Zion

Linic Z., Pripravi srce za susret, Zagreb, 1995.
Prepare Your Heart for the Meeting

Manjackal J., Molitva cini cudesa, Zagreb, 2004.
Prayer Creates Miracles

Manjackal J., Dodirnuo me i ozdravio, Zagreb, 2005.
He Touched and Healed Me

Manjackal J. Eureka, Zagreb, 2001.
Eureka

Manjackal J., Molitve koje ce promjeniti tvoj zivot, Zagreb, 2001.
Prayers That Will Change Your Life

Manjackal J., Nas Bog je silan Bog, Zagreb, 2001.
Our God is Mighty

Manjackal J., Udjimo u korablju, Zagreb, 2001.
Let Us Enter the Ark

Marcelic J. Anneliese Michel i zli duhovi, Jelsa, 1997.
Anneliese Michel and the Evil Spirits

McKenna S., Cudesa se dogadjaju, Jelsa, 1998.
Miracles Do Happen

Milingo E., Licem u lice s djavlom, Zagreb, 2000.
Face to Face With the Devil

Miskic I. Gospodine, ozdravi me, Zagreb, 2001.
Heal Me, Lord

Monbourquette J., Kako oprostiti, Zagreb, 1997.
How to Forgive

Moser G., Tisina usred buke, Korcula, 1978.
Silence in the Midst of Noise

Muhlen H., Novi susret s Bogom, Jelsa, 1994.
New Encounter With God

Muller J., Demoni medju nama, Djakovo, 1998.
Demons Among Us

Muller J. Proklet, opcinjen, poludio ili nesto drugo?, Mostar, 1998.
Cursed, Obsessed, Insane or Something Else?

Musolesi A. Presidenete degli esorcisti: esperienze e delucidazioni di don
Gabriele Amort, Ravena, 2005.

Nanni G., Il dito dio e il potere di Satana: l'esorcismo, Libreria editrice vaticana, 2004.

Oropeza B. J., O andjelima , demonima i duhovnom ratovanju, Zagreb, 2001.
About Angels, Demons and Spiritual Warfare

Offedu L.; Sansa F., I ragazzi di Satana, Edizione Saggi, Milano, 2005.

Papinsko vijece za medjureligijski dijalog: Isus Krist-donositelj vode zive.
Krscansko promisljanje o New Age-u, Split, 2001.
The Pontifical Council for Interreligious Dialogue: Jesus Christ, The Bearer Of The
Water Of Life. A Christian reflection on the "New Age"

Pertisko T. Zalost, zrtva i trijumf, Zagreb, 2000.
Sorrow, Sacrifice and the Triumph

Petersdorff E. Demoni, vjestice, spiritisti, Split, 2001.
Demons, Witches, Spiritualists

Porcarelli A., Spiritizam, Osijek, 2000.
Spiritualism

Primorac P. Dim sotonin, Trogir, 2004.
Smoke of Satan

Psel M. O demonima, Split, 1995.
About Demons

Ratzinger J., Sol zemlje, Zagreb, 1997.
Salt of the Earth

Degli R., Esorcismi e preghiere per circostanze particolari, Libreria editrice vaticana, 2001.

Salemon B., Molite da ozdravite, Jelsa, 1995.
Pray to Be Healed

Salvucci R., Le potenze malefiche, Edotrice Shalom, Camarata Picena (An), 1998.

Salvucci R., Cosa fare con questi Diavoli, Ancora editrice, Milano, 2002.

Sodi M. Tra meleficio, patologie e possessione demoniaca, Padova, 2003.

Sullivan F. A:, Karizme i karizmatska obnova, Jelsa, 1984.
Charisms and the Charismatic Renewal

Tardif E., Isus je prisutan, Jelsa, 1993.
Jesus is Present

Tardif E., Isus me ucinio svjedokom, Jelsa, 1991.
Jesus Made Me a Witness

Tardif E. U vatri ljubavi, Jelsa, 1996.
In the Flame of Love

Tosatti A., Inchiesta sul Demonio, Casale Monteferrato, 2005.

Vinkov I., Opsjednutost i egzorcizam, Zagreb, 2004.
Obsession and Exorcism

Vjera i zdravlje — Zbornik, Zagreb, 2005.
Proceedings of "Religion and Health"

Vukman Z., Propast svijeta ili novo doba poganstva, Split, 1998.
Demise of the World or a New Era of Paganism

Wenisch B. Satanizam, Djakovo, 1993.
Satanism

Zakonik kanonskog prava, Zagreb, 1988.
Code of Canon Law